Dancing
With Your
Horse

Dancing

With Your

Horse

Revised Edition

Libby Anderson and Leigh Ann Hazel-Groux

Based on the original edition by
Mary Campbell

Half Halt Press, Inc.
Boonsboro, Maryland

Dancing with Your Horse, Revised Edition

© 2003 Half Halt Press, Inc.

Published in the United States of America by

Half Halt Press, Inc.
P.O. Box 67
Boonsboro, MD 21713

www.halfhaltpress.com

Jacket and book design by
Diane Hill Turrell, DDH Design
Tunkhannock, PA

Horse illustration on cover by Dorothy Smith

USDF Freestyle Score Sheets used by the kind permission
of United States Dressage Federation.

FEI Intermediate and Grand Prix Freestyle Score Sheets
used by the kind permission of the Fédération
Equestre Internationale.

Library of Congress Cataloging-in-Publication Data

Anderson, Libby.
      Dancing with your horse / Libby Anderson and Leigh Ann Hazel-Groux.-- Rev. ed.
        p. cm.
      "Based on the original edition by Mary Campbell."
      ISBN 0-939481-66-9
        1. Musical freestyle rides (Dressage) I. Hazel-Groux, Leigh Ann. II. Campbell, Mary
   E., 1924- Dancing with your horse. III. Title.

   SF309.6.C35 2003
   798.2'3--dc22
                                                                                    2003060358

Table of Contents - Dancing With Your Horse

Acknowledgements

The authors wish to thank all the wonderful folks who aided and assisted in the research and publication of this tribute to the late Mary Campbell. It has taken more than a village of friends and mentors to produce this book.

First, thanks to Half Halt Press and Beth Carnes, who was the inspiration for initiating this revision of Mary Campbell's original *Dancing with Your Horse*, which was first published in 1989. For this we are very grateful. It has been an amazing experience to work on the book and document the growth of the musical freestyle over the past 15 to 20 years. Mary would have been amazed to know of the incredible growth in the musical freestyle and would share our joy in knowing the future of the musical freestyle is secure, both on American soil and also on the global scene.

This book would not have been possible without the direct help and encouragement from the United States Dressage Federation and its staff, particularly Marsha McCleney, Program Coordinator for the USDF, who assisted in many aspects of fact-finding for the book. The USDF Dressage Freestyle Committee headed by Ann Guptill was most helpful in directing research for the book to particular targets. Thanks also to individuals on the Committee, Terry Ciotto-Gallo, Sandy Howard, Michael Matson, Tigger Montaque and Jeff Ashton Moore, for their invaluable help in the development of the book.

We'd also like to thank USA Equestrian for its support in the publication of the book, as well as Mariette Whitages, Chair of the Dressage Committee of the Fédération Equestre Internationale, and Linda Zang, FEI "O" Dressage

Judge for the USA, for their help with current rules and regulations of the sport. Thanks also to Liz Serle, Kay Meredith, Trip Harding, Anne Gribbons, Marlene Whitaker and many other unnamed individuals whose assistance and enthusiasm helped to bring this book to fruition.

Thanks also to Dorothy Smith for designing the wonderful artwork for the cover, Diane H. Turrell for her design help and advice, and John and Roslyn Langlois for their technical expertise.

Last but not least, many, many thanks to our families and friends who have borne with us during this intensive writing, editing and research period.

Foreword by Kay Meredith

Many of us got into dressage in the first place just so we could ride a freestyle. For more years than I care to count, I have ridden, judged and watched rides to music at all levels. During those early years, the Detroit area was a hotbed of riders brave enough to try the musical freestyle. I clung to the sidelines and watched enviously at those courageous souls vying to win the Col. Kitts trophy. "How wonderful," I thought, "to have a horse trained to do changes every stride, piaffe and passage. All this put to music!"

Why do I say "brave?" Because there were not any written rules at that time relating to the freestyle. We just put in the movements we did best and hoped for the best! Eventually that was no longer allowed—but it was fun while it lasted!

All art forms—which is where I place freestyles— undergo an evolution which begins with the primitive and progresses to the sophisticated from we see today. Now, the rules for the musical freestyle are firmly established and riders and trainers are educated to suitable music and choreography. We are encouraged to be brave and innovative, without sacrificing overall quality.

As Linda Zang so succinctly noted, today the freestyle goes into a bright future with all the rules and regulations it deserves. More than that, a freestyle done well at any level is respected as much as its parallel test without music.

The freestyle is here to stay and our sport is better for it.

Foreword by Anne Gribbons

*M*any years ago, I wrote the foreword to Mary Campbell's book about how to create a freestyle. At the time, she was truly a pioneer, working with what we today consider primitive means to accomplish a lot with less technology, less information and less support than is available to the freestyle enthusiast of today.

We have indeed come a long way since Mary did her work, and I am delighted to read this extension of her efforts. This new work by Libby Anderson and Leigh Ann Hazel-Groux is much more extensive, more sophisticated and more encompassing than Mary's original book. As such, it will be helpful and inspiring to new generations of riders and supporters of the freestyle.

I enjoy seeing the growth and development of riding to music, and I welcome this book as a step forward in the process. But I can also look back and say to myself, "Thank you, Mary, for the inspiration and the courage to get us started."

The late Mary Campbell

A Word of Introduction

An older definition of musical freestyle read something like this: "The rider is to create and ride from memory an original ride that shows her horse to his best advantage. In the freestyle, creativity and artistic presentation as well as technical execution will be considered."

This simple definition describes one of the fastest developing areas of competition in equestrian sport, the musical freestyle, sometimes referred to as a *kür*. It's not hard to understand why. The sight of a horse and rider dancing their way through choreography of technical craftsmanship set to music is beautiful and inspiring, a true celebration of harmony between rider and horse. There is a magical quality to it.

The value of the musical freestyle to the sport of dressage cannot be underestimated. It does for dressage what ice dancing has done for skating, in bringing new spectators to the sport. Where all too frequently the spectators at a dressage competition were mostly family, grooms and other participants, we now see non-horsy spectators flocking to shows and taking a great interest in musical freestyle rides. With the growing popularity of these rides, classes are now performed at all levels, beginning with USDF First Level through FEI Grand Prix.

This book will explore and explain the art form that is musical freestyle and discuss both its history, its creation and look to its future. It is by no means a definitive tome on the subject, just as there is no one way to create a freestyle. However, we, the authors, hope to take the work begun by Mary Campbell and expand upon it as she desired in order to help others gain a better understanding and appreciation for the sport.

To gain a better understanding of the requirements for this musical performance, let's look closely at dictionary definitions:

Free: Not confined to the usual rules or patterns – in a free manner. Not subject to restraint, at liberty, independent, self-deciding, without obstruction, without charge, unconfined. Able to move in any direction.

Style: A manner of doing, a distinctive or especially admired manner of expressing thought. A distinctive or characteristic manner. Overall excellence, skill, or grace in performance.

Freestyle: Sports not limited to a specified style or pattern of movement.

These definitions suggest how innovative the horse and rider team can and should be. The requirements in musical freestyle competition emphasize technical skills, superb music and choreography, and artistic presentation. The demands placed on the horse are for the gaits, strength and obedience. When there is a weakness in a ride, one or more of these seven elements is lacking.

An interesting note about the word *kür*, which is also used to refer to this musical performance: Although the word has been used in this context for a long time, its derivation seems to be a mystery. The origin is German, but German dictionaries list nothing related to either horses or music: courting, love, teaching, health, to elect or to exercise at discretion. Perhaps it evolves from this last definition in some way. In this book, we use the term musical freestyle as the United States Dressage Federation (USDF) and the USA Equestrian (USAE) use it.

It must be noted at the outset that there is no compromise of classical dressage in the art of musical freestyle by setting the movements to music. Consider the following:

1. An extended trot is a beautiful sight to see.

2. A *correct* extended trot is not only beautiful, but also inspirational.

3. A *correct* extended trot set to music is not only beautiful and inspirational; it is a celebration for the senses of seeing, hearing and feeling.

It is as important in the freestyle as in the regular tests that the transitions and movements of the performance be correct and true.

To be able to create a musical freestyle ride, you do not have to be greatly concerned about complex theories of music. You do not even have to be particularly musical to get a great deal of enjoyment from creating a musical ride with your horse. While it would be super if you were able to go to a musical show and come home and play all the tunes, have absolute pitch, and recognize the note A when you hear it, it is not a requirement for creating a freestyle ride. No one can listen to a piece of special music without sooner or later being invaded, as it were, by the beat. The music takes hold with snapping fingers, tapping feet, or clapping hands. If music can do this to you, you have the ability to be a freestyle rider.

And what about your horse? Does it naturally have the ability to dance? The whole question of "do animals dance?" is an interesting one. Many primitive peoples take for granted the correspondence between the movements of animals and the choreography of the dance; this notion is often incorporated into their own dances by imitation. Animals often seem to be performing dances when they are wooing a prospective mate (or fighting over one).

Most people, however, would reject this as simply a projection of a strictly human activity onto animals. Your horse cannot dance with you in the same way that another human would. Much of the performance of the musical freestyle reflects adapting the music and the choreography to the horse, rather than the other way around.

One thing is clear, however: your horse will respond to the musical freestyle in a way you have probably never felt before. It may be that because you as rider-director are responding to either the feeling the music gives you and the horse follows, or because your rhythm becomes more consistent while you ride to music, but there is no doubt that there is a visible effect on the horse. This is one of the joys you have awaiting you as you learn more about the musical freestyle.

Chapter 1

Presenting the Musical Freestyle

Libby Anderson

A Brief History

Throughout history, our friend and partner, the horse, has served us well as a means of transport, both in war and in peace, and as a ready source of meat, skins and milk.

With the tapestry of time unfolding, civilization began to change. From hunter-gatherers to farmers to community-orientated populations that worked together for a common good, mankind entered the modern world characterized by agricultural, industrial, scientific and information revolutions, peppered with power-seeking wars and natural catastrophes.

The bond between man and horse continued to grow stronger and more secure with this ongoing world development. Due to the wider and more specialized roles horses were taking on, man began breeding and selecting horses to better suit these different goals. Even before the time of Austrian monk Gregor Mendel, who developed the fundamental principles that would become the modern science of genetics, horse breeders tinkered with selective breeding to develop horses that were suitable for pulling, racing, war, transport, pleasure and performance.

In addition to the normal domestic uses for the horse, such as transportation for both people and goods and a practical means of tilling the soil and harvesting the produce, yet another avenue beckoned: the use of the horse for recreation and celebration. Man's love of pomp, ceremony and tradition naturally led to the use of the horse as a vehicle for artistic expression in the form of exhibitions, parades, victory celebrations, ballets, entertainment and other festivities. Many of these spectacles were accompanied by music—live bands, drums, vocals and an assortment of sound to enhance the performance and beauty of the horse.

Horses performed in small groups such as pas de deux (two horses), pas de trios (three horses) and quadrilles (typically four or eight horses), as well as a part of large assemblies performing complicated choreography to music provided by full orchestras. These large shows were known by various names, including circus, ballet and carousel, and were held in great exhibition halls, in palace gardens, on church properties and in town squares—anywhere folks normally gathered to celebrate festivities or tragedies.

As the huge, intricate and beautiful musical performances of the 1600s dwindled in Europe due to the great financial cost and the ultimate impossibility to outdo the magnificent performances staged in Vienna, smaller productions gained in popularity. Beginning in the 1800s, quadrilles, musical rides, parades, circus and exhibition rides grew more popular as they were less costly to produce, took up less space and provided amusement. Both the rich and nobly bred and the general public could view some of these productions, though the latter from a lesser vantagepoint.

The circus gained popularity in more recent years, and the horse became a star performer due to humans' innate love for watching horses at liberty, dancing and performing tricks—all legitimate forms of entertainment. The modern circus was invented by Philip Astley and originally was centered around the horse. Astley emulated the trick riders of the time and opened Paris' first circus (named for the circular ring they performed in) in 1782. Unfortunately this role of the horse was not always monitored for the horse's well being. Horses risked death and injury during their exciting performances such as walking on their hind legs, diving off a hundred foot tower into a small tank, performing balancing acts and working with live wild animals such as lions and tigers. It did, however, fulfill the human desire to continue the magic relationship with the horse.

Birth of the Musical Freestyle

Dressage—which is a French word that simply means "training"—is one of the oldest of the equestrian disciplines. It is steeped in history and was well documented around 400 B.C. by the Greek historian Xenophon. Often referred to as "the father of dressage," Xenophon wrote down, in considerable detail, his teachings and principles for training the horse. Unlike those before him, his methods were humane, and much of his basic teaching is still valid today. This is astounding considering today's world of shortcuts and easy answers.

Throughout history, horses were used for many purposes including fighting wars for their masters. Dressage training taught the horse to assist his soldier/rider to win tournaments, battles and wars. The horse was taught to piaffe and passage in order to inflict damage and evade the enemy. The "airs above ground" were useful both in war and for performance. The levade raised the rider up above the enemy so he could get a good view of the fighting. The mounted warrior performing the courbette and capriole presented a fearsome and alarming picture to the enemy as the horses hind hooves smashed down on their opponents' bodies. In addition, the horse had to be able to gallop fast and maneuver easily to evade the enemy.

The historic past and the exciting present join hands and unite to celebrate the horse today. Institutions such as the Spanish Riding School, the Cadre Noir and the Andalusian

School carry on these ancient traditions to this day. The Spanish Riding School in Vienna, Austria is one the oldest of such institutions where the art of classical riding is still carried on in the old tradition. The Spanish Riding School was built by order of Emperor Karl IV (in 1729). His portrait still stands in the great riding hall and is saluted daily by all the riders at the School. Here the art of "Haute Ecole" and classical dressage training has continued despite minor disruptions such as world wars for the past 400 years.

In the twenty-first century horses are no longer used for battle, or as means of transport. Horses now are categorized as sport horses, for the pleasure of their human masters or under the general title of "for recreational uses." The sport of dressage has followed a similar route as other sports and art forms that have been forced to adapt to modern times such as ice skating, ballet, opera and gymnastics to remain current. For dressage, this transition has been a slow one, and one that has endured many growing pains.

Competitive dressage has never been a great spectator sport. It is often perceived as elitist, boring as watching paint dry (particularly at the lower levels) and, generally speaking, a slow-moving sport with few exciting moments. For devotees, dressage competition is stirring stuff, but for the general public, who basically are horse lovers or at least horse fanciers, the sport is not addictive enough to fill the grandstands or attract lucrative sponsors. In modern competition, the dressage horse performs several of the classical figures and maneuvers, that have been deemed appropriate by the Fédération Equestre International (FEI) or the USAE, for the level that the horse is competing. For the uninitiated spectator watching a horse perform these movements, in the official standard arena of 60 by 20 meters, one can understand that without informed commentary the spectacle may look rather baffling. In addition the spectators are requested to remain silent for the duration of the dressage test. In other equestrian sports such as polo, racing and western reining the spectators are free to applaud, hoot and holler to their hearts content.

One of the ways dressage has been made more spectator-friendly is through an artistic dimension of classical dressage—the musical freestyle. Following the old traditions of parade and carrousel, dressage champions have been performing pas des deux, pas des trios, quadrilles, and single exhibitions of classical dressage movements set to music in order to draw the public's attention to the sport. The late Dr Reiner Klimke of Germany, Anne-Grethe Jenson Törnblad of Denmark, Gabriela Grillo of Germany and Jennie Lorenston-Clarke of Great Britain, among others, have thrilled audiences with spectacular musical performances. Horse enthusiasts were delighted with these exhibitions, and many lovers of ice skating, ballet and other arts have been drawn to the excitement of this rediscovered art form. The musical presentation tells a story that the audience can follow and appreciate. The beauty of the horses, the harmony shown between both the individual horse and rider combinations and the group as a whole, and the magic of the musical background are all essential ingredients in any good performance. On completion of the performance the audience can show their appreciation by clapping heartily. Even hooting and hollering are allowed!

Appreciating the value of the addition of music to enhance a dressage performance, the FEI and interested individuals began to look into formalizing the musical freestyle into a recognized competition format. As early as the 1980s the FEI expressed a reserved enthusiasm for the musical freestyle partly because it was so popular with not only the "horsy" set, but indeed, it was also appreciated by the general public. In addition, there were murmurs from the Olympic Committee as early as 1992 that dressage may be dropped from the Olympic agenda. This was probably due to a general lack of interest by the media, lack of spectator appeal and the high cost for countries to fly equine combinations to competitions. The FEI followed through with this interest and incorporated the musical freestyle into accepted national and international competition. By this means the FEI attracted more sponsors, media attention and spectators to the sport of dressage and insured that the dressage competition was continued as an Olympic event.

The FEI was also closely following the new developments taking place in the sports of figure skating and gymnastics and used some of these ideas, such as electronic timing, instant results and the addition of a new appealing format of a freestyle to music, to incorporate into their new musical freestyle format. The FEI could see that these sports drew in an enthusiastic audience. These additions would prove a useful model to follow to make dressage, which had begun to attract many enthusiastic spectators and sponsors, even more spectator and "user-friendly." They found that part of the spectator allure of these sports was the initial visual thrill of watching fast-moving and daring figures combined with instant electronic feedback of the judge's scores. This helped create and maintain spectator interest throughout the competition. The FEI and many members of the dressage community could see the musical freestyle creating such spectator interest in their own sport.

One of the first staunch advocates to the idea of a freestyle to music was the late Duke of Richmond who held the first of these *kürs* at his lovely property "Goodwood" in the late seventies. Another principal individual in the development of the freestyle was Mariette Withages, who was a member of the World Cup Committee from the early days to 1995. Today, as Chairman of the Dressage Committee of the

FEI, she continues to judge and support the musical freestyle in all international events. We must also mention Joep Bartels as an historic figure in the formation of the World Cup. In his book The World Cup Dressage (1995, printed in Holland by Drukkerij Oldemarkt), he tells us that after the initial years when both spectators and sponsors had been won over, the major source of resistance came from riders and trainers, particularly the German riders and trainers! "It took almost ten years to convince all the top riders and certainly their trainers that the *kür* to music was the guarantee for a prosperous future." Another founder and supporter of the musical freestyle was Wolfgang Niggli who, as chairman of the FEI Dressage Committee, promoted the concept of a World Cup for the freestyle. Mr. Niggli was not only an international dressage judge but also an experienced judge of figure skating. In 1994 Volvo became a sponsor for the first World Cup held in 1985. This was a great success, with 4,000 spectators giving accolades and congratulations to the FEI and the Volvo sponsor.

When Nashua took over the sponsorship in 1987, the FEI rules were still evolving with changes being made once a weakness in the rules became apparent. In 1987 Nina Menkova showed some stunning circus type moves such as multi-pirouettes (including an about turn) and her compatriot Yuri Kovshov showed some piaffe backwards. These were loved by the crowd but were soon declared forbidden movements by the FEI Dressage Committee who quickly made any "circus" moves illegal.

During these years the FEI Dressage Committee and various national dressage federations were planning and improving the rules and regulations to make future competitions fair for the horse and rider, exciting for the audience, well suited for the television and multi-media format, and to ensure that the idea of "circus" was not associated with the development of the musical freestyle. The FEI was determined to keep the musical freestyle in a classical dressage format so the quality of the basic training of dressage would not be compromised. These new and evolving rules, to this day, prevent competitors from asking their horses to perform movements that may be detrimental to their health and well being.

In a span of less than 20 years, the musical freestyle has become a significant part of the Olympic Games, World Championships and World Cup Finals. The result has packed grandstands, attracted wonderful sponsors and provided amazing freestyle competition to delight the entire equestrian world.

The Development of the Modern Musical Freestyle in Europe

The idea behind adding a freestyle competition to FEI competition was actually born in the United States in 1984 during the Los Angeles Olympics. Joep Bartels and his wife Tineke noticed the crowd's reaction when Reiner Klimke and Ahlerich performed perfect one-tempi changes to the rhythm of the Olympic theme during his victory lap after he won the gold medal. By the next year, the musical freestyle became an accepted international event when Bartels created a new league based on the freestyle concept called the World Cup. The first World Cup Final was held in 's-Hertogenbosch, The Netherlands, in 1986.

In this new league, horses were required to perform a compulsory Grand Prix test with the top 12 horses moving on to perform musical freestyles in the reverse order of their placing in the Grand Prix. In fact, the first year, only 12 riders competed and therefore all participated in both the Grand Prix and the musical freestyle ride.

The initial sponsor of the World Cup was Nashua from 1984 to 1990, and Volvo took over for the next decade. Without these staunch and loyal sponsors the future of the musical freestyle would have been in doubt. Indeed, the inclusion of the *kür* in the Olympic Games and World Championships is partly due to the successful sponsorship of the musical freestyle and the dedicated efforts of past FEI dressage committee chairpersons Wolfgang Niggli and Eric Lette and current chairperson Mariette Withages.

The early winners of the World Cup have also made history in the development of the musical freestyle. The first winner in 1986 was Anne-Grethe Jenson Törnblad of Denmark riding the talented Marzog with a soft, classical performance of high technical excellence. Other winners who followed included Swiss rider Christine Stückelberger and her successful partner Gauguin de Lully who thrilled the crowds for two consecutive years. Margit Otto-Crépin of France and Corlandus won the 1989 final and Sven Rothenberger, riding under the German flag, aboard Andiamo was the 1990 winner.

In the 1990s came some fabulous, innovative and incredibly talented horse-and-rider combinations who used new and complicated freestyle patterns, all within the FEI rules and guidelines. Among these are Finland's Kyra Kyrklund and the superstar Matador, and Germany's Isabell Werth and the temperamental mare Fabienne, who wowed the audience with music from The Beatles. Monica Theodorescu, also of Germany, and the big, black gelding Ganimedes won the World Cup on two successive years to the music of Oklahoma. Next it was Dutch rider Anky van Grunsven's turn to win three consecutive World Cup Finals riding Cameleon Bonfire. The last Final sponsored by Volvo took place in Los Angeles, CA and was won by Anky van Grunseven and Olympic Bonfire to packed crowds.

After BCM took over the sponsorship of the Final in 1999, Van Grunsven returned to win the next two Finals, setting a record of five World Cup Final wins. Germany's Ulla Salzgeber and the Latvian-bred Rusty have two consecutive wins of the World Cup Final. Always in tune with modern trends to maintain public enthusiasm and consolidate sponsors, the World Cup continues to transform itself. At the 2002 Final in The Netherlands, for the first time, the freestyle results determined the winner of the Final. The Grand Prix was still compulsory, but the scores only determined the order of go for the Freestyle.

The inclusion of the musical freestyle in international competition was an overwhelming success, and the European Championships added individual medals based on scores from the Grand Prix Special and Freestyle in 1991. This formula was used again in 1993 and changed to its current format at the 1995 European Championship where scores from the Grand Prix, Grand Prix Special and Freestyle are averaged for final scores. This formula has carried over into the 1996 Olympic Games and continues to be used today.

The Development of Musical Freestyle in the United States

Initially, the United States had some catching up to do to improve the training, riding and breeding of the dressage horse to be competitive with their international cousins across the Atlantic. However, by the year 2002, the United States has reached a competitive edge regarding dressage competition both at home and abroad.

As early as the 1960s, American dressage enthusiasts were putting together great scores to music and performed these musical freestyles in exhibitions all over the country. Chuck Grant, Kit Young, Jessica Ransehousen, Kay Meredith,

Kay Meredith on Domino. *Photo courtesy of the Dressage Foundation.*

Lendon Gray, and Linda Zang, to name just a few, contributed to the development of the musical freestyle in the United States.

During this time USAE (then called the American Horse Shows Association (AHSA)) and the USDF encouraged competition in the musical freestyle and developed rules and regulations for conducting musical freestyle competitions at recognized dressage shows. By the 1980s the musical freestyle was firmly established in the dressage competition circuit. Early stars in freestyle were Dianna Rankin, Robert Dover, Jessica Ransehousen, Hilda Gurney and Jeff Moore.

Parallel with FEI rules, AHSA and USDF developed rules for musical freestyles in the United States. Lower level freestyles appropriate to AHSA First, Second, Third and Fourth Level dressage tests were offered at competitions, and rules were being developed and upgraded as happens in any new discipline. Today, the regulations are well established, and the musical freestyle is offered at recognized dressage shows and freestyle spectaculars all across the country.

Freestyle classes are open to all dressage riders and enthusiasts. This includes a growing number of disabled riders worldwide. Riding for the disabled is under the auspices of the International Paralympic Equestrian Committee (IPEC). IPEC offers both compulsory and musical freestyle tests for all four grades of disabled riders. American disabled freestyle riders have done very well on the local and international scene.

It was an exciting year for the United States when the 1995 World Cup Final was held in Los Angeles, California— the first time in its history it was held outside Europe. With much fanfare and publicity, this prestigious event was heralded as "Dressage Goes Hollywood." And with Hollywood efficiency, the organizers went about producing a professional World Cup Final that thrilled audiences, created interest for more sponsors and put the United States on the international dressage scene as a major player.

In 1996, the year of the 100th Olympiad, the Olympic Games were held in the United States in Atlanta, Georgia. These were the first Olympic Games where the musical freestyle was incorporated into the format for the individual competition. America's team, which included Guenter Seidel, Robert Dover, Michelle Gibson and Steffen Peters

Robin Brueckmann on Bordeaux in an FEI exhibition ride at Devon. Note that Bordeaux is bridleless.

Photo courtesy of Terri Miller.

claimed the bronze medal. The United States proved beyond a shadow of doubt that as a nation they are indeed competitive in all the aspects of classical dressage including the musical freestyle.

As a testament to the growing popularity of musical freestyle in the United States, the year 2002 was declared the "Year of the Freestyle" jointly by USDF and USAE. Much time and effort went into developing an exciting program of musical freestyle events and competitions to celebrate the year. Among the many events, which included the first-ever U.S. Freestyle Championship, USDF hosted a spectacular Freestyle Symposium, which included many horses and riders in a musical theater with the theme of *The Lion King*. This was in addition to many panels and workshops, all for the purpose of discussing and enabling all interested riders to create their own musical freestyles. Perhaps this is the first of many such symposiums.

Without a doubt, the musical freestyle is here to stay.

Chapter 2

The Judge's Perspective

Libby Anderson

From the time the rider enters the arena at A to the final salute, he or she attempts to relate a musical story to the judges and spectators. The interpretation of this musical story is up to the rider and/or choreographer, but magic can be woven into the theme so that both judges and spectators are drawn into the spell.

It is always interesting to view the musical freestyle from the judge's perspective. The competitors, trainers, choreographers and spectators all have their own perspective on the judging of the freestyle from their particular vantagepoints. Sometimes the opinion varies. All of the many and varied participants involved in developing a freestyle need to understand how the judge goes about awarding points and scores for the musical performance as well as having an understanding of the marking of both the technical and artistic work.

Before we begin this discussion, remember that the judge is always on the rider's side and is hoping to see and enjoy the best performance possible from that particular competitor. The judge's job is to award appropriate marks and give helpful comments for both the technical and artistic sections of the musical freestyle. By studying these comments, you can improve the standard of your musical freestyle and achieve the ultimate goal of dancing with your horse.

Judging a Freestyle

The dressage judge uses several of his senses to evaluate freestyle performances. The eyes see the movements and help in judging the overall appearance and attitude of the horse and rider. We may see the swishing of a tail and ears that are flat back. We may see the soft back and rounded outline of a willing, happy and contented horse. We can also see the poor rider lacking balance and empathy with the horse. In addition, the ears can hear the grinding of the teeth, the swishing of the tail, the irregular or regular footfalls of the horse and any sound that the horse and/or rider may make such as a whinny or a voice command. The sense of touch is more an instinct for a judge who at times can almost feel the soft connection with the reins and the swing of the back.

Former FEI Dressage Committee Chairman Wolfgang Niggli once said: "A judge needs to see with the ears and hear with the eyes." Take the example of a horse grinding his teeth in a competition, Mr. Niggli knew that although he could hear the grinding of teeth, he could also see that the mouth was soft and foamy, the ears are forward and that the back is swinging. In that case he would not hear the grinding. If however, he saw that the back was tense, the mouth dry and the ears back, of course he heard the grinding!

The job of the dressage judge is to objectively assess the musical freestyle on both its technical execution and artistic impression. When designing a freestyle, the choice of music and choreography is important, but it is imperative to focus on the technical correctness of every movement ridden in the kür. If the technical segment is weak, say, averaging marks on the judging scale of 4's (insufficient), 5's (sufficient) and 6's (satisfactory), it is hard to justify high marks in the artistic section as to a degree the artistic section is linked with the technical work.* If the technical aspect is good, say a mark of 8 on the judging scale which indicates above average, or fairly good, a

---

* Note that the judging scale is the same for the freestyle as regular dressage tests. The scale can be found in the **USAE Rule Book,** Article 1922 No. 7.

mark of 7 on the judging scale, this segment will receive above average or good marks from the judge. If the artistic impression is also exciting, suitable and imaginative, you have the potential for a good overall score. However, if some technical sections are weak or deficient, it is impossible to score the artistic impression highly, particularly in the first two sections on the artistic side. These marks relate to rhythm, energy and elasticity and harmony between horse and rider. A poor technical performance will be unable to score highly in these sections. Even with terrific music the horse will not look good performing poor movements. The judge can comment that the music was pleasing and suitable and suggest that the rider improve the technical side for improved marks.

The USDF musical freestyle score sheet is divided into two sections (see Appendix 1 for sample score sheets). The first is for Technical Execution and the second is for Artistic Impression. The Technical includes all movements that are normally encountered in the straight USAE dressage tests for that level. For example, take the Fourth Level Freestyle. Movements that are clearly forbidden are:

1. Full canter pirouette,
2. Tempi changes of two's and one's.
3. Piaffe.
4. Passage.

If the rider shows movements that are above the level (forbidden), they will incur a deduction of four points for each forbidden movement from the total score for Technical Execution, but not for each recurrence of the same movement. All figures and patterns, combination or transitions composed of elements permitted in Fourth Level are allowed, even if the resulting configuration is found in higher levels.

The dressage judge will judge all the movements presented in the Fourth Level Freestyle as if it were a regular dressage test.

Of course, if the music is great and the unfolding story is fascinating, often times the judges can be excused if they find themselves tapping out a rhythm with the feet and smiling at a particularly appropriate sequence!

The Artistic Impression contains five sections. The first two of these are involved with the quality of the musical freestyle itself, that is, a mark for "rhythm, energy and elasticity" and a mark for "harmony between horse and rider." The other three marks are related to some of the other essential components of the musical freestyle. These include choreography, use of arena, inventiveness, design cohesiveness, balance, ingenuity and creativity. The fourth mark is simply for the degree of difficulty. The fifth and last mark is for choice of music and interpretation of music.

The total marks for Technical Execution add up to the same number of marks as for Artistic Impression. In the case of the Fourth Level freestyle, the Technical marks add up to 120 and the Artistic add up to 120. Overall there is a balance of the marks divided between the Technical and the Artistic sides. The judge must accurately access the technical marks, which is fairly routine for a qualified judge, and evaluate the Artistic side, which is still related to the Technical for the first two marks. The FEI level musical freestyles are also balanced the same way between Technical and Artistic. The total marks for the Intermediate 1 Freestyle Test is 400, divided evenly between the Technical and the Artistic.

Technical Scores

Though the musical freestyle gives riders more freedom to express themselves, it cannot be overlooked that in order to perform a good freestyle that will receive good, generous marks from the judges, the horse must first show solid dressage basics.

There are no shortcuts or easy answers in the technical

requirements of the freestyle. While good music and choreography can accentuate a test, they cannot cover up for poor basic training. Even put to the best of music, a half pass with no bend will not look good. An insufficient shoulder-in that lacks engagement and shows resistance will look even worse when set to music. Also, if a horse shows some irregularity in the basic gaits during the musical freestyle, no music can mask that fact. Remember the judge sees with the ears and hears with the eyes. He can see and hear the irregularity. Thus, the technical marks will suffer, and the first two artistic marks will reflect this recurring problem.

The technical execution of the musical freestyle is judged just as a regular dressage test. The regular dressage tests from for Training, First, Second, Third and Fourth levels are published by USAE and are the standard tests performed at all dressage shows. These tests are scored for the execution of different movements appropriate to the level of the horse. For example, at Second Level the horse must be able to perform shoulder-in, travers, medium trot and canter and a turn on the haunches at the walk.

In addition, the USAE has a rule regarding qualification for the musical freestyle in Article 1928 No 9:

Except at USAE/USDF Championships, in order to enter a freestyle class at any USAE/USDF level, a horse/rider combination must have competed in the highest test of the declared freestyle level or any test at a higher level with a minimum score of 58% at an USAE recognized show. A photocopy of the test verifying eligibility must be submitted with the entry for the freestyle class.

The rider must be secure in the execution of all the technical requirements at the highest test of the level (i.e., First Level, Test 4 in a First Level freestyle) in order to successfully add the elements of music and choreography.

If the technical section is weak, it is difficult to gain good marks in the artistic section because the first two marks of the artistic section are related to the technical section. For example, it is impossible to receive good artistic marks for rhythm and energy if the performance was sleepy or lazy. Resistance and a lack of basic communication between horse and rider shows a clear lack of harmony between horse and rider and will be reflected in the artistic marks in addition to the technical marks.

Artistic Scores

The artistic section of the musical freestyle evaluates the suitability of the music to the individual horse and how well it accentuates his type, movement and personality, as well as choreography, degree of difficulty and risk.

The artistic section has five individual marks with coefficients assigned to them:

1. Rhythm, energy and elasticity.
2. Harmony between horse and rider.
3. Choreography. Use of arena. Inventiveness.
4. Degree of difficulty. Well-calculated risks.
5. Choice of music and interpretation of music.

The judge's score for each mark is multiplied by the coefficient, therefore, the higher the coefficient, the more that particular mark is weighted in the overall score for the test. The coefficients assigned vary depending on the level of the freestyle. In the case of a tie between two competitors for a placing in a musical freestyle the tie is to be split by taking the highest score in the artistic score.

The last three marks in this section are often the most frustrating for the rider as these represent less tangible aspects of the ride—the magic and skill of the kür itself. If the music and choreography work, the rider is amply rewarded in these sections. The rider and choreographer need to develop skills relating to the music, phrasing (a musical phrase may be used to lead into an extension or a transition), rhythm, use of arena and, last but not least, blending the movements to the music and to the horse's personality.

The choreography, use of arena space and inventiveness all relate to how successful the rider and choreographer are in developing the "story" of a *kür*. As this has a coefficient of 4 in the FEI and 3 in the USDF musical freestyles, this becomes very important in determining the overall result.

The Importance of Choreography in Judging

Choreographing a successful freestyle is not as easy as it appears, especially at the lower levels. It requires skill and diligence in researching some of the other known rides at your level, knowing your own horse's strengths and weakness, riding various interesting movements allowed in, say the First Level Freestyle. These moves can be tried in different spots in the arena to evaluate the visual impact. It may be helpful to video some of these movements and visualizing how they will all fit in with the music. It is important to make good use of the entire arena with moves that are clear and easy to interpret. You will develop an understanding of the musical nuances interwoven in your individual *kür*. As the rider proceeds up the levels it still is not a simple process to be original and inventive. There are, however, more degrees of freedom to integrating choreography, degree of difficulty and well-calculated risks with the interpretation of the music.

Judges like to see riders use all of the arena space in a non-test-like manner. This means that riders should avoid repeating circles, loops, serpentines and teardrops ad nauseam, particularly when the freestyle at that level does not require it. These types of additions often make the choreography look boring and tedious.

The degree of difficulty and well-calculated risks can be

incorporated at all levels of freestyle. At First Level, transitions on the quarter line and across the diagonal add to the normal degree of difficulty for the level. Leg yield zigzags and lengthening down the centerline or across the short diagonals can add to the expression of the freestyle. At Third Level, there are more options for the degree of difficulty with flying changes, half pass, medium and extended gaits all awaiting expression and execution. At the FEI levels, the degree of difficulty takes on new meaning; interesting and inventive movements sometimes show really spectacular risk-taking incorporated within the theme of the freestyle.

Examples abound when watching World Cup Dressage competitions. Some of the exciting risks include one-handed canter zigzags, extended canter to double pirouettes down the centerline, one-handed pirouettes in both directions, tempi changes on a curved line, and passage half pass to trot half pass to passage half pass.

However, from the judge's standpoint, it never pays to try to execute a movement that is particularly difficult for your horse. You risk losing everything if your horse becomes flustered, uncomfortable or disobedient. The horse must be confident and comfortable with all the movements required in the freestyle. It is advisable to ride the musical freestyle at a level you know that both you and your horse will feel comfortable. This may require that you design your *kür* one level below the level you are competing. According to the **USAE Rulebook**, you can compete at a lower level freestyle as long as it is only one level down from your usual level in straight dressage, as long as you have fulfilled the requirements for that level. For example, a Third Level horse will feel comfortable performing all Second Level movements and will be able to take risks at the Second Level *kür*. This should make for good marks at the Second Level Freestyle. If the same horse is doing a Third Level Freestyle, it may be better to avoid too many difficult movements that could cause problems in the performance.

When a musical freestyle performance gives spectators and judges "goose bumps," it means that that the technical and artistic score are in harmony and that, for a few minutes, the judge is drawn into the private world of the particular horse and rider combination. The musical story they weave before him, the flawless precision of pattern execution and the correct technical work will all meld into one beautiful moment in time.

Rules and Requirements

It is the rider's responsibility to be familiar with the rules and requirements for the level of freestyle he or she is riding. The requirements for First through Fourth Levels are available from the USDF, and the international level rules (Prix St. Georges, Intermediare I and Grand Prix) are available from the FEI (copies of which can be had at the USAE and the USDF). The addresses for these organizations are found in Appendix 2.

Some things to be particularly aware of are time requirements and time limits, and movements and combinations of movements that are allowed or prohibited at any given level. Rule changes are ongoing as the development of the musical freestyle continues to evolve. It is up to the rider to keep abreast of these changes. It is a good idea to attend the annual USDF convention each December, which includes updates and discussions on musical freestyles as well as new rules or proposed rule changes. In addition, there are several freestyle seminars held around the United States throughout the year.

Chapter 3

A Musical Freestyle Primer

Libby Anderson

Many dressage riders, as they realize their goals in basic training, look to the musical freestyle to express the beauty, individuality and freedom of their discipline. In addition, the dressage community in general tends to gather in riders from all equestrian disciplines. One perhaps obvious reason is that dressage riding can be successfully carried out until the rider reaches old age or senility! The sport of dressage itself benefits from this diversity as many of the good riders come from eventing, western, endurance, polo, pony club and jumping, and all bring their particular skills to the sport. The musical freestyle allows riders from so many different backgrounds to express their musicality and ingenuity as they weave a musical story, which defines them as a horse and rider combination.

Dressage Basics

Part of the magic of the dressage musical freestyle is that two individuals are involved. By comparison, in individual figure skating and gymnastics, an individual performs. The addition of the horse to the musical freestyle equation adds an unknown factor. Horse and rider must have achieved correct basic training so that these two individuals are capable of working as a team. This is not as simple as it would first appear and requires years of work, training, understanding and dedication to perform a musical freestyle that both the horse and rider enjoy as well as providing entertainment to spectators and a pretty portrait for the judges.

This book does not cover basic training of the horse and rider. However, this training cannot be by-passed if you wish to perform a successful musical freestyle. I always remember the simple training philosophy of my mentor, the late Franz Maringer, who was the Chief Rider at the Spanish Riding School in Vienna and, later, Australia's Olympic Coach:

1. *Ride forward and straight*, and,
2. *Ride on your line and at your speed.*

Maringer often said that dressage principles should be simple and natural for the horse and rider. However, these principles are deceptively difficult to attain although we should all continually strive for them. That said, it should be clear that the dressage rider who wishes to excel at the musical freestyle must spend time and effort in correct training.

Riding To Music

Now the rider and trainer can begin to plan a musical freestyle at the level, or the level below, which the horse and rider are competing. We want to make the performance comfortable for the horse and not add too much degree of difficulty in executing the movements. The rider has enough to worry about with all the technical aspects and musicality without stressing the horse to perform movements that are already difficult for him.

Begin to get the feel of the freestyle by riding and training regularly to music. Any music you enjoy and that you feel may have possibilities for your horse is good to start with. After riding to music on a regular basis, you will have a better idea as to which music suits the rhythm and the personality of your horse. Even if you never follow up with riding a musical freestyle in competition, you will notice the benefits that riding to music brings to you and your horse. Your horse will respond noticeably to the musical phases, pick up a trot as the beat dictates and relax and concentrate more on the job in hand. This may be, in part, the result of your response to the feeling and harmony of the music. Your rhythm may become more consistent as you ride to music. Simply riding to music will have a visible and lasting effect on both horse and rider. This is just one of the joys awaiting the rider as you progress up the musical freestyle path.

Developing the Freestyle

Once you are ready to begin developing a musical freestyle, your first goal is to choose good music. It should be music that you enjoy and want to work with and the music must fit all three gaits of your horse. The music you choose should also suit your horse. If you have a dainty and elegant horse, choose music to suit the horse's personality. It should not be too powerful and strong, as this will bury your horse deep in the musical phases. Do not choose any music that makes the horse look too light, weak or wimpy. There is a wonderful range of terrific music for all sorts of horses. For the elegant horse there is an abundance of musical scores from classical, film themes, folk and patriotic music. If your horse is heavy set and powerful, choose music to highlight his good features. Well-planned choreography put to good musical phasing can appear to lighten up most horses and create an impression of controlled energy without heaviness. The more experience you have in creating the freestyle and working with different music, the better you will be at finding just the right music for your horse. As previously said, the music you choose must also be music that you enjoy. A child will choose different music than a teenager, and a young adult will choose different music than an older person. You

Sue Blinks and Flim Flam at the 2000 Sydney Olympics.
Photo courtesy of Diana de Rosa.

Well known musical freestyle rider Sue Blinks and her horse Flim Flam demonstrate just how interwoven the music and choreography can be to produce a moving and breath-taking freestyle. Flim Flam is a very elegant and elastic horse so Sue chose music with feeling and sensitivity to help tell the musical story of her freestyle. The music was from the Cirque du Soleil, and magically drew the audience in the web of the story, while the choreography increased the tension level as Flim Flam demonstrated all his excellent features such as his straight flying changes and his unbelievable rhythm in the piaffe which seems to be so effortless, and his 21 one-tempi changes on the last centerline. The result is a complete and balanced musical freestyle, a joy to watch and a pleasure to judge.

You must choose music that you enjoy and want to work with.
Alison Head and Calhombeque perform their beautiful freestyle.
Photo courtesy of Diane Boyd.

will live with the music you choose for a good while, so
choose well. You will enjoy all the painstaking work ahead
of you to bring the musical freestyle to fruition.

Once you are happy with the choice of music, the
freestyle must stand on its own as a musical performance.
The freestyle should not be a jumble of unrelated pieces
from unrelated orchestras. This creates a disharmony and
lack of continuity. Try for the same genre of musical pieces.
All classical, all pop, all film themes or all folk. You will be
surprised just how much opportunity you have to develop
all the gaits and movements from the same music genre.

The final freestyle is a sequence of moves and figures showing variation both within the gaits and between the gaits. The music must define changes within the gait. The trot extension is a dramatic and powerful movement; the half pass is more light and airy which can set your foot tapping. The same notion applies to the canter, where the canter pirouettes are a quiet and isolated moment in the freestyle, the tempi changes are rhythmic and the half passes are lilting and light. If you can close your eyes and listen to your completed freestyle music you should be able to see in your mind's eye all the different gaits and all the variations within the gaits. Once you can do this you know that you have put together a fabulous freestyle where the music tells the story and the music matches both you and your horse as regards rhythm and personality. Good Luck!

tempo can occur from slow to fast by a change in diet, weather, footing, environs and/or health of the horse. If these variations happen, the rider must take notice and make the necessary adjustments to correct the tempo. This can become one of the most important factors in an effective performance of a musical freestyle as once the music is determined and recorded, success of the freestyle artistically depends upon staying with your music's beat.

Tempo, as the rate of speed or movement, is also the rate of repetition of the rhythm. This can also depend on the horse's make-up, such as conformation and temperament. However, no matter what the individual tempo of the horse, it must stay the same while going around the arena, into corners, moving laterally across the ring and throughout circles. The horse should not speed up or slow down within any given gait. It is the rider's responsibility to make corrections necessary to maintain a true tempo.

There are commonly employed musical terms for degrees of tempo. Traditionally—but not always—the terminology is in Italian. Here are a few in order from slowest to fastest. Where do you think your horse fits in?

- **Largo** – very slow and broad
- **Adagio** – very slow
- **Lento** – slow
- **Andante** – "walking" tempo; implies a slow, steady movement
- **Moderato** – moderate tempo
- **Allegro** – quick, fast
- **Vivace** – spirited
- **Presto** – very fast

As you can see, the terms describing the different shades of tempo have positive meanings but are open to various individual interpretations as each horse will have his own measure of speed.

There also are relationships between tempo terms frequently used that are predominately descriptive, but convey the "character" of the horse:

- *Maestoso* – majestically, slow to moderate tempo
- *Tranquillo* – calmly
- *Grazioso* – gracefully
- *Animato* – animated
- *Scherzos* – in a jesting, playful manner
- *Con fuoco* – with fire; fast or very fast tempo
- *Con brio* – brisk, lively

Throughout this book, when we use the word tempo, it can apply to the horse as well as to the music. Understanding and keeping tempo applies to horses and riders at any level. Sometimes people will use the terms rhythm and tempo interchangeably. However, though they are intimately interrelated, they are nonetheless independent variables. Having a clear perception of each will help you to choreograph and orchestrate your musical freestyle ride.

Remember that **rhythm** is the pattern of the beat (e.g. rhythm of the gaits), while the **tempo** is the speed of the pattern.

As we continue our discussion of music theory, we begin to get into the more detailed questions of how to determine beat, how to time the horse and music, and how this all works together to design a musical freestyle ride. Let's start with the basic question:

What is a Beat?

Many years ago military leaders determined that when a soldier was marching and took a full step or pace (i.e. left, right, left) he would cover approximately one yard. To keep a consistent cadence (or beat) they used drums with a heavy emphasis on the "downbeat" (each time the left foot hit the ground). This showed that a steady cadence or drumbeat of 130 downbeats per minute would have them cover one mile in approximately 13 minutes. Hence, most march music is played at 130 beats per minute. If you have ever marched in a parade, you can recall counting "left ... left ... left-right-left," putting the emphasis on the left foot to coincide with the downbeats of a bass drum.

This was the practical use of downbeats per minute. In freestyles, we are faced with a similar—but more complex—problem due to existing variables: Horses come in all different sizes, with each having his own tempo and moving at different downbeats per minute. In addition, the rate of downbeats per minute can change as a horse becomes more collected and developed.

In music, the amount of time a note is held is measured in units and that is what is called a beat. A beat is a regular pulsation like the ticking of a clock. Conductors indicate the beat to an orchestra by the up and down movements of the baton.

There are sounds in beat patterns such as the two-beat, in-and-out pattern of breathing, the lub-dub of heartbeats, waves, skipping, clapping, and, of course, dancing. Added to all of these are the wonderful sounds of hoofbeats—the music to riders' ears.

Beats can be compared to tapping your foot in an even and steady manner. The same goes for a horse. Watch someone ride and follow the movements of one forefoot of a horse in trot. Do you see the tapping? When tapping, two motions are required: down and up. Therefore, each beat has two parts—or halves: a downbeat and an upbeat. Each time you tap your foot (the downbeat), a number is counted starting with one, and each time the toe is raised (the upbeat), the word "and" is said. As shown in the first illustration, try

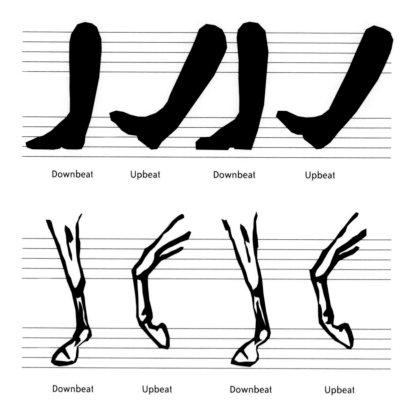

| Downbeat | Upbeat | Downbeat | Upbeat |

| Downbeat | Upbeat | Downbeat | Upbeat |

tapping and counting the down- and upbeat. Now look at the next illustration of the front hooves of the horse: There is a repeat of the tapping—the downbeat and the upbeat.

As you continue watching the horse and rider for a few minutes, notice that your eyes see the motion of the hoof and will set your foot in motion to keep in time. Your ears hear the footfalls of the horse's hooves. You observe that the rider feels the beat by following the motion of the horse with his or her whole body. Therefore, the eyes, the ears and the body are all engaged in the concept of the beat.

Components of Music

Measure, Bar Lines and Double Bar Lines

Written music is divided into equal parts called measures. On a sheet of music, this is the distance between two vertical bar lines. Double bar lines, one thin and one thick, show the end of a piece of music. How the music is written within these lines will determine how it is played, and therefore how it will sound.

Note Values

The time intended for a note to sound is indicated in writing by the shape and appearance of the note and by additional stems, flags and dots that may be attached to the note. The whole note is the basic value against which all other values are measured. The illustration shows several ways the whole note can be subdivided:

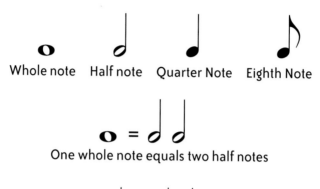

Whole note   Half note   Quarter Note   Eighth Note

One whole note equals two half notes

One half note equals two quarter notes

One whole note equals four quarter notes

One whole note equals eight eighth notes

A dot after a note (.) adds one count, which prolongs the value of a note by half of its original value. For example, a dotted half note (♩.) equals three counts.

The next illustration is a visual method of comprehending these relationships:

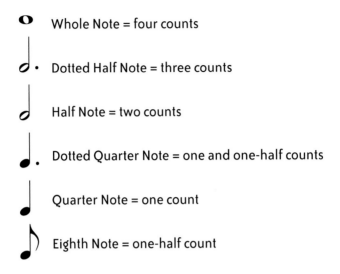

Whole Note = four counts

Dotted Half Note = three counts

Half Note = two counts

Dotted Quarter Note = one and one-half counts

Quarter Note = one count

Eighth Note = one-half count

Each note that is encountered in music has a definite time value. If you study the illustrations of note values, you can compare them to a 12-inch ruler. The ruler is marked in inches with fractional parts measuring specific lengths. So it is with music notes measuring lengths as indicated by their form.

Here is another way to look at notes and their values:

Time Signatures

A time signature is a fractional sign placed at the beginning of a piece of music. There is a top number and a bottom number, i.e., 4/4. The top number indicates the number of beats (or counts) in each measure. The bottom number shows what kind of note gets one beat. In 4/4 time, for example, there are four beats in each measure and the quarter note gets the beat.

In $\frac{4}{4}$ time there are four beats in each measure.

A whole note receives four beats.

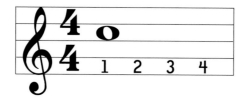

A half note receives two beats.

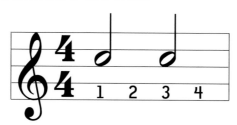

A quarter note receives one beat.

The walk is a four-beat movement.

In **2/4** time, there are two beats in each measure, and each quarter note gets the beat.

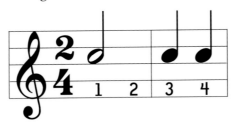

The trot is a two-beat movement.

In **3/4** time, there are three beats in each measure, and each quarter note gets the beat.

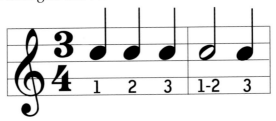

The canter is a three-beat movement.

To sum up this brief music theory lesson, remember that each note has a definite length of time or beat, just as each footfall of a horse can be measured for length of time or number of beats. Compare the illustrations with the rhythms of the horse: two beats for trot, three beats for canter and four beats for the walk. This concept of beats will appear again and again throughout this book as this is part of basic music theory for counting beats per minute.

This next illustration shows the different rhythms of the horses' gaits in musical form:

The Trot Rhythm of the Horse

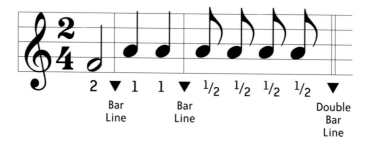

The Canter Rhythm of the Horse

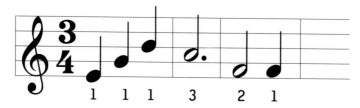

The Walk Rhythm of the Horse

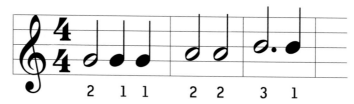

Phrases

The word "phrase" is an important word in music. Understanding phrasing can make a significant difference in the quality of your musical freestyle.

Think of music as language. When we express our thoughts in spoken language, we do it by using words. To convey our feelings in music, we use tones instead of words. Since music is divided into logical sections, it can be compared to a sentence in a speech, or equivalent to punctuation marks in written language. Just as a sentence is divided into smaller parts of speech (phrases and clauses) by commas, colons and so forth, a musical sentence is also divided by measured movements into phrases. When we hear a story, we listen to it sentence by sentence. When we listen to music, we listen phrase by phrase. Hence, musical sentences are called phrases. In short, phrasing is punctuation applied to music.

In music, a phrase is a short musical thought at least two, but typically four, measures in length. A phrase is the natural division of a melody. Only when the notes are arranged into musical sentences do they take on a definite meaning.

Like any language, music is a combination of phrases. If you tell a story or recite a poem, you don't stop in the middle or part way through a phrase. Music will have the same effect if you stop without finishing a musical phrase. This holds true with or without words. For instance, if you were singing the nursery rhyme "Mary had a Little Lamb" and only sang, "Mary had a little lamb, little lamb, little …," without finishing the phrase, there is a definite sense of being incomplete. But when you finish the line "… lamb," there is a completion of the phrase that allows the flow into the next line of the song.

This concept of phrasing will be important as you begin to select and edit the music for your freestyle. Variations in music and the ending of musical phrases can be used as a signal to indicate a transition or change within movements or between gaits. They will allow you to develop a flowing, fluid ride without abrupt stops and/or changes that could jar your audience and judges.

Chapter 5

Getting Started

Leigh Ann Hazel-Groux

How to Determine and Use Beats Per Minute

*B*eats per minute is the key to uniting the components in this method of developing a musical freestyle. Using beats per minute as your guide, you will learn to time the horse, the music and select the correct music for each of your horse's gaits. Horses cannot "dance" with you—at least not in the same manner as a human—so by using this theory, you will adapt the music to the horse. This is what will give the delightful feeling and visual impression of horse and rider "dancing" together.

The word "beat" in this context refers specifically to the downbeat. This is the beat where everything starts. Visualize the conductor of an orchestra, baton raised, all musicians' eyes on him as he brings down the baton emphatically on the first note—or downbeat—and the orchestra plays.

As the conductor moves the baton, there is always one emphatic downbeat repeated at even intervals. This is the tempo, or the measure of speed. When you tap your foot or clap your hands to music, you almost unknowingly emphasize the downbeat.

The famous bandleader Lawrence Welk was often kidded about his distinctive method of starting the band by tapping his foot, moving his hands up and down and saying, "a one and a two." What he was actually doing was setting a tempo for very danceable music. To further analyze this little ritual of his, I will put the heavy emphasis on the downbeat:

"a ONE and a TWO and a ONE and a TWO." You can readily see where the downbeat fits with the upbeat in between ("and a").

In Chapter 4, we discussed the basic gaits (rhythm) of the horse and their related beats. Now we will learn to count the rate of speed—the tempo—of each of the gaits. First though, let's look at the various timing tools available for counting.

Timers

How you keep time is a matter of preference. Before making a large investment in one of the many timekeepers available, do some shopping where you can handle and try out a variety of timers to in order to select the one most suitable for your needs.

You can probably go right to work and do well with a wristwatch or a simple household clock with a second hand. However, as you become more involved in working with musical freestyles, more sophisticated equipment will be an asset. Just as a carpenter needs a variety of tools for his trade, a person who designs musical freestyles should have instruments for a well-done finished product.

There are many different types of timers available, which can be found at any good music store. Here are a few you might encounter:

Metronome

A metronome is a timepiece invented in the 19th century. It makes a ticking sound for any speed at which it is set, from one to more than 200 beats per minute. In its simplest form, it has a clockwork device with an inverted pendulum that beats time at a rate determined by the position of a sliding weight on the pendulum.

Wind-up metronomes, such as the type described

above, produce audible sounds, while electronic models flash lights and/or intermittent sounds at any desired musical speed. Both are especially useful to help a person working with music to maintain a regular tempo. The metronome setting indicates the exact number of beats per minute and precisely notes the tempo.

Modern metronomes run on batteries and come in pocket sizes with quartz movements, earphone jacks and switch selections that let you hear the beat and see it on a digital display. The electronic metronome is probably the best investment for this purpose because it operates in any position, is small enough to be taken out into the arena and is unlikely to have an uneven beat. Some versions are as small as a credit card and can fit in your pocket. By setting them at a given tempo with sound, you can hear the beat and use this as an aid to learning to ride in a given tempo.

Stopwatch

A stopwatch accounts for elapsed time in split seconds, seconds, minutes or, in some instances, hours. It has a hand that can be started and stopped at will by pressing a small button on the watch. There are spring-wound as well as elaborate electronic stopwatches. There are also models made specifically for sporting events, including eventing. These also can be quite functional in timing beats per minute of the horse.

A stopwatch is not only useful in helping to determine beats per minute of horse and music. It is very helpful when putting your freestyle together and tracking the timing of each gait section as well as the overall length of the freestyle. But we'll discuss that in more detail in a later chapter.

Counting Beats Per Minute

There are various ways to put together a musical freestyle ride. Some riders choose their music first and ride the horse to it and develop their choreography as they go. Others develop the choreography first, and choose and edit their music to match their patterns.

Riders who have never performed or put together a freestyle may find that learning to time the beats per minute of the horse and adding the music is the easier way to get a handle on the process. For the more "musically challenged" rider, learning to count the beats per minute takes some of the mystery out of the process and, therefore, designing a freestyle becomes fun instead of scary or unnerving.

To determine the beats per minute of your horse, you need a stopwatch or a watch with a second hand and, ideally, an unmounted helper who is familiar with the horse's gaits.

The tempo of a horse's gaits often differs between when he first starts working and after he is warmed up. Therefore it is preferable for the horse to be somewhat warmed up before timing as it will give a truer picture of the attitude and tempo of the horse. Some horses maintain the same tempo coming out of the stall, going to work and continuing into collection. There are others that will start working in a hurried frenzy and settle into a steady tempo. A third type of horse is sluggish to start and must be pushed into the correct tempo. Twenty minutes is the approximate time needed to determine the beats per minute.

The average range of beats per minute for each gait are

- **Walk**—50 to 66 beats per minute
- **Passage**—60 to 64 beats per minute
- **Trot**—76 to 88 beats per minute
- **Canter**—96 to 108 beats per minute.

A horse can still be correct even if his gaits fall outside these beats per minute ranges. A small pony, for instance, will have a faster tempo than a larger horse. Also, as you will see, you will need to double-check your tempos once your horse is fully warmed as they may change once the horse is working.

Timing the horse and timing the music are very similar to taking a person's pulse. When a nurse checks a patient's pulse, she watches the second hand of a watch as she counts the number of times the patient's heartbeats in one minute. This same method is used to determine the beats per minute of a horse's gaits. As the horse travels in one direction, use the inside front foot (for example, when going to the left, it would be the front left foot) to act as a guide in determining the beats per minute of all gaits. I use only one foot to watch to simplify things. You can actually count each front foot as it strikes the ground, but if you are inexperienced, it can make counting a little more complicated. If you prefer to count this way, simply double the beat numbers noted above. For example, counting one front foot at trot for one minute equals 78 beats per minute. If you count both front feet, that number would double and would equal 156 beats per minute. However, for purposes of this book and the method described here, we only are counting the inside front leg.

It will be necessary to time each gait several times to ensure accuracy. It's best to time the walk after working at the trot or canter. The walk can be a difficult gait. If the horse is stiff or older, the walk will become freer after his muscles loosen at the trot or canter. In addition, any tenseness that might be reflected in the walk at the beginning of a work session is usually relaxed by the end of it.

After you have checked your beats per minute several times, you will have determined the median tempo for that horse at that particular gait. Write down the numbers for the beats per minute each time you time that gait. It will look like this: trot—78/80/81/78/78. These figures indicate that the horse started to work slow, got quick and settled into a rhythm—the most consistent tempo being 78.

In the beginning, it might be helpful to have an assistant on the ground count the beats per minute of your horse during a lesson with your instructor to make certain your horse is in his true working gaits. You will be amazed after working with the music how inconsistent a horse's tempo can be. As the rider, you are the regulator of the tempo. Some horses need correction often and using the music as your guide can improve your whole schooling program—but more on that in another chapter.

The Video Timing Method

There is another method of timing that I want to mention. Having an assistant videotape you riding your horse at all three gaits can also help you count the beats per minute. In addition, you can use this tape later when you have selected music to see how well it matches your horse's gaits. However, a word of caution: VCRs can have slightly different playback speeds, so be sure to double check your beats per minute "live." The same goes for riding to music to test it. What might look good on videotape might not necessarily work when actually riding to it. Again, you need to do a live field test.

Using videotape is also helpful in deciding between styles of music because you can see for yourself what your horse looks like set to different types of music. Have a friend record your working session with the music playing in the arena. When you play it back at home, you can evaluate it as a watcher, not just as a rider.

Now let's look at all three gaits and count the beats per minute for each. We'll begin with the trot, because it is the easiest to work with, and begin to understand how to use this method.

The Trot

The **USAE 2003 Rule Book**, Article 1904, says

1. *The trot is a gait of "two-time" on alternate diagonal legs (near fore and right hind leg and vice versa) separated by a moment of suspension.*

2. *The trot, always with free, active and regular steps, should be moved into without hesitation.*

3. *The quality of the trot is judged by the general impression, the regularity and elasticity of the steps—originated from a supple back and well engaged hindquarters—and by the ability of maintaining the same rhythm and natural balance even after transition from one trot to another.*

To determine beats per minute of the horse at a trot, the person with the timer must be at a good vantagepoint to watch the movement of the horse's legs. It is often easiest to work the horse on a 20-meter circle, first to the left, and after several timings have been taken, to the right. The person timing should first practice just watching and counting each time the inside forefoot strikes the ground. Then, using a stopwatch, the assistant counts how many times the inside forefoot strikes the ground in one minute. This number is the number of beats per minute of the trot. A slightly easier way is to count the number of times the inside forefoot strikes the ground during 15 seconds, and multiply by four to get the number of beats per minute. Remember to take the timing several times in each direction to ensure accuracy.

Sometimes the beats per minute will vary from one

direction to the other. This usually corresponds to the "soft" and "hard" sides of the horse as he will go faster or slower depending on whether he is supple or stiff in that direction. The rider will have to make a determination as to the tempo in which the horse is best balanced and supple and use that number. An instructor can be very helpful in making this determination.

Again, check the beats per minute several times to ensure accuracy. This is extremely important at all gaits and especially as the horse progresses in his training. As the horse changes, physically and athletically, the number of beats per minute may change, and the rider may need to make adjustments in either the choreography or the music.

Keep in mind that what you are doing is determining the tempo, or time, which will be the basis for bringing together all of the components for a successful freestyle to music. Remember, the trot has one downbeat and one up beat. The emphasis here is only on the downbeat: DOWN-up-DOWN-up.

The Walk

As stated in the **USAE 2003 RuleBook**, Article 1903

1. *The walk is a marching gait in which the footfalls*
   of the horse's feet follow one another in 'four-time',
   well marked and maintained in all work at the walk.

When the four beats cease to be distinctly marked, even and regular, the walk is disunited or broken.

It is at the walk that the imperfections of dressage are most evident. This is also the reason why a horse should not be asked to walk "on the bit" at the early stages of his training. A too precipitous collection will not only spoil the collected walk but the medium and the extended walk as well.

To determine the beats per minute of the horse at walk,

follow the same procedure as the trot. The walk is a four-beat movement. The horse will have either two or three feet on the ground simultaneously depending on what stage of the gait he is in, and there is no period of suspension as in the canter and trot. When performed with regularity, you will hear four distinct and even footfalls.

As in the trot, ask the horse to walk on the left rein first. The person timing with a stopwatch will count the number of times the left forefoot strikes the ground during one minute. This number is the beats per minute of the walk. The most common range for the walk is 50 to 66 beats per minute.

The Canter

According to the **USAE 2003 RuleBook**, Article 1905

1. *The canter is a gait of three-time, where at canter to the right, for instance, the footfalls follow one another as follows: left hind, left diagonal (simultaneously left fore and right hind), right fore, followed by a moment of suspension with all four feet in the air before the next stride begins.*

2. *The canter always with light, cadenced and regular strides, should be moved into without hesitation.*

3. *The quality of the canter is judged by the general impression, the regularity and lightness of the three-time pace originated in the acceptance of the bridle with a supple poll and in the engagement of the hindquarters with an active hock action and by the ability of maintaining the same rhythm and a natural balance even after a transition from one canter to another. The horse should always remain straight on straight lines.*

To determine the number of beats per minute of the horse at a canter, follow the same procedure as outlined for the trot and the walk. This gait is a three-beat movement with a moment of suspension. The canter is correct when three hoof beats can be heard and the horse bounds elastically from the ground and returns to it unchanged.

As with the trot and walk, your helper on the ground should watch the inside forefoot, counting how many times it strikes the ground in one minute. The most common range for the canter is 96 to 108 beats per minute.

A note on the tempo of music for the canter—since the canter is a gait of three-time, you could say it is in 3/4 tempo, however, 4/4 music can also work quite well as the moment of suspension fills out the beat, though silently.

Piaffe and Passage

Ideally, passage and piaffe should be in the same tempo. It is easier, however, to time the passage and use that number for both. You time the passage exactly as you did the other three gaits. An interesting note is that the beats per minute of passage will normally be approximately 20 beats per minute less than the trot. For example, with a trot of 84 beats per minute, you can expect the passage to be about 64 beats per minute. The general range for passage is 60 to 64 beats per minute.

Now that you have an understanding of timing the beats per minute of the horse, we can proceed with learning the beats per minute of the music and learn how the two will be united. As you will see, the methods of determining the beats per minute of the music are very similar to determining the beats per minute of the horse.

Timing the Music

While it is not a written rule that the music match the beats per minute of the gaits of the horse, this is, in fact, one of the things the judges are looking for in a well done freestyle. Music that matches a horse's gaits, as well as his or her personality, is what helps to make it truly look as if horse and rider are dancing to the music—a picture that is enjoyed both by those watching and the horse and rider "dancing."

In much the same manner as we learned to time beats per minute of the horse, we will now go through the procedures for timing music. The instructions and terminology for timing music are very similar to that of working with the horse. The materials you will need are a recording of the music that you will potentially use, a stopwatch, a watch with a second hand or a metronome and a pencil and paper.

When first selecting music for your freestyle, keep it simple and familiar without vocals. A strong, emphatic downbeat will help you hear the tempo. Initially, this doesn't even have to be a piece of music you will ride to but just one to help you get the feel of listening for the beat of the music.

Instead of watching the horse's hoof strike the ground on the downbeat as we did in timing beats per minute of the horse, you will listen for and tap your foot or your hand to the rhythm of the music to measure the speed—or tempo — of the music to determine the beats per minute. As discussed earlier when determining the beats per minute of your horse's gaits, the downbeat is where everything starts. The downbeats of the horse's three gaits have a parallel existence to music. You count the downbeat of the music to determine the beats per minute of the music.

As you begin to listen, don't be concerned at first with counting. Simply tap the beat with your hand or your foot.

Once you are comfortable with tapping the beat, there are several ways you can measure the tempo of the music.

The first way is to use a stopwatch, or a watch with a second hand, just as you did when counting your horse's gaits. Once you are familiar with a piece of music, start the stopwatch and count the downbeats for one minute. This will be your music tempo. Again, you can also count for 15 seconds and multiply by four, but check your music throughout the piece as tempos can change as the piece progresses.

A second method is to use a metronome with a sliding pendulum. As you listen to the music, keep adjusting the metronome until the downbeat of the music matches the downbeat of the metronome. This is the beats per minute. It requires practice and concentration to coordinate the beat of the metronome and the music.

Another method uses an electronic metronome with a digital readout and a "tap" button. You can tap out the downbeats on the button and the metronome will automatically compute the beats per minute. Then, you can set it on continual beat play and check it against the music for correctness.

You can also use the metronome for selecting music if you have a lot of music to time and are looking specifically for a piece with a particular tempo (for example, you need music at 80 beats per minute). Set the metronome at 80 beats per minute and let the music play. You can do other chores while the music is playing at the same time the metronome is ticking. As soon as a musical tune is played in the tempo that you have set on the metronome, you will hear the two matching downbeats. Make a note of the song and tempo for future reference.

After you've done the above steps, you can see that learning to time music is a simple as listening and counting. Anyone can learn to do it. Once you have begun to understand this, it is time for the next phase—selecting the music for your own freestyle ride.

Chapter 6

The Music

Leigh Ann Hazel-Groux

Selecting music for your freestyle is a time-consuming job, but it can also be a very exciting adventure. Make sure you leave yourself plenty of time and don't start this project with only days or weeks to go before your competition, otherwise, you will end up frustrated. Plan on putting in approximately 80 hours of work from start to finish—from selecting the music to planning the choreography to the final editing of your cassette or CD.

In general, it makes no difference if you plan the choreography for the freestyle first or if you select the music first. The top competitors are split almost 50/50 on how to begin. Some like to plan the choreography first to make sure the movements will show their horses to the best of their abilities and fit the music to it. Others prefer to begin with the music and let the phrasing of the melody "suggest" the choreography. Whichever method you use, there's plenty to be done, and you probably will be working on both parts independently as well as together.

It is a good idea to keep it simple when you are first starting out. It's also best to use music that is familiar to you, and that you have timed and found to have the correct beats per minute for your horse at all three gaits. In addition, the music should make you feel comfortable, happy and "in sync" with your horse.

You may also discover that your horse prefers a certain style of music. (Yes, they do pay attention!) On more than one occasion, I have watched a horse seem very indifferent to one piece of music but "light up" when a different style was played. One horse I know of became quite grumpy with loud, "electric" music but became quite energized when classical music was played. Remember that the horse is your partner and you should listen to his input!

Choosing Your Music

Creating and presenting a musical freestyle involves many decisions that culminate in the horse and rider being presented to their best advantage. Therefore, the selection of music for your freestyle is central. The suitability of music to horse and rider will "set the stage" for the freestyle, and it will be instantly reflected in the special relationship it sets into motion as horse and rider prepare to dance.

Musical suitability means what you hear matches what you see. This is so important that it is part of the scoring of the freestyle (see "Musicality" on the score sheet). Suitable music will enhance the horse by complementing his size, personality, breed and movement. Ideally, the music will show and match the versatility and athletic prowess of the horse as well as the ingenuity of the rider in the creativity of the choreography presented in the ride.

It may seem obvious that the horse has a big role to play in the freestyle, but many times he seems to be forgotten. You must remember to consider you horse as your dancing partner as you work to identify the music. The piece that you have in mind may, in truth, not be the piece that fits and shows off your horse to his best.

I was once asked to ride a demonstration for a tour group from the Smithsonian Institution that was viewing horse farms and wineries. My thought process went like this: "Smithsonian...museum... classical group ... classical music." But it didn't work that way. Every piece I thought would work did nothing to enhance my horse or show us to the best advantage. I finally selected some New Age-style music that worked so well that when a friend, who is a FEI judge, watched the video afterward, she laughed and commented that it even made my horse—a tall, heavy Oldenburg—look light. In fact, he looked and acted downright impulsive! Conclusion: predetermining your music before you make some trial rides to it may not be for the best. Be open and consider various styles. You may be very surprised.

When choosing your music, ask yourself the following questions:

1. Can you feel the music and say, "How wonderful it *feels* with my horse?"

2. Do you *like* the music? Music that feels good and is in correct tempo is essential but, if for any reason, a certain type just turns you off, forget it and try something else. Remember, you are going to hear this music *a lot*.

3. Can you present the music? When you find music that makes you feel good and you like it, start thinking in terms of the dazzling presentation you can make with it.

4. Ask yourself, "What do I want from my music?" Are you looking for a particular "mood," a certain "feel" or, as a friend of mine once said, "music that will make an audience sit up and take notice?"

Listen to and work with a lot of music. Write down the names of the pieces that seem to jump out at you. Then make a tape with different style possibilities at the correct tempos for each gait, and just let it play as you ride to it. Ask friends to watch while you ride and give you their input—even if they aren't "horsy." It's amazing, but when the music and horse are right for each other, you don't necessarily have to know horses or dressage to appreciate it. If you have a regular instructor, be sure and get his or her help and input also.

Above all, *take your time*. It takes time and patience to put together a good freestyle. Freestyles become a very personal expression of us and of our horses. Just remember, have fun with the process. It's an adventure and a journey, and it's only just beginning.

Styles of Music

The ultimate success of your freestyle depends on the proper selection of music that shows off you and your horse to the best of your combined abilities. Once the best music is selected, the work of choreography and "honing" your ride becomes much easier.

Fortunately—or perhaps, unfortunately—there is quite a wide variety of music to choose from, comprising many different styles. "Style" in music refers to a characteristic way of using melody, rhythm, tone, color, dynamics, harmony, texture and form. Music such as jazz, march, waltz, patriotic, big band, etc., all have their own basic plans. The particular way these elements are combined results in a total sound that is distinctive.

While the following list is in no way meant to be all inclusive, it will give you a good idea of some of the more well-known styles of music that often works well for freestyles.

Folk Music

Some of our most beautiful music comes, not as you might suppose from the pens of famous composers, but from folk tunes, which have been passed down through generations. Folk music exists in every culture in the world and tells the stories of human experiences. There are work songs, love songs, cradlesongs, drinking songs, war songs and laments, to name just a few.

Because of its charming simplicity folk music is enjoyed by people from myriad nations and walks of life. It deals with human experience and reflects the musical preferences of the individual regions and peoples. Many folk tunes will endure forever as masterpieces of melody and they are often incorporated into larger works by better known composers.

The term "folk music" covers a large variety of types of music including Irish, Spanish, Russian, polka and blue-grass. With its simplicity, melodic patterns and even tempos, folk music is worth investigating. Folk music often shows different national styles very clearly through its use of melody and specific instrumentation that is indigenous to the culture. With an understanding of the national "styles," you will be able to be more precise in planning and selecting music for the freestyle when you want to express a certain mood. Good resources for this type of music can be found at your local library, public radio station or even a large music store chain, such as Tower Records.

You will also find that these national musical traits influence style. French music is likely to be sophisticated with a rhythmic, light beat, while German music is apt to be vigorous with a sturdy rhythm and thick texture. On the other hand Russian music often runs the extremes of loud, soft, fast and slow, and has mixed and less-common meters. Italian music is usually vital and rhythmic with a more marked beat, emphasis on melody and the added beauty of the voice (although as has been noted, the use of vocals in not encouraged). Irish music has become very popular of late with the dance troupe *Riverdance*.

Latin Music

Latin music is a lot of fun to ride to. It is very lively and had good rhythm. Music from some artists such as Herb Alpert or Brazil 66 have steady beats and make good choices, especially for newcomers to the art of freestyle where a distinct, regular beat makes the tempo easier to hear and, therefore, follow.

Jazz

Jazz is a unique style of music that emerged in the United States in the latter part of the 19th century, primarily around New Orleans. The term "jazz" was first used probably around 1915 and has been applied to various forms since then, including "Dixieland," "Chicago style," "be-bop," "progressive," "swing" and "free jazz." Characteristics of jazz music include steady but strongly accented rhythms, usually played by a rhythm section consisting of drums, double bass or tuba, and a piano. Often there is improvisation by soloists within a given piece.

A more recent form of jazz is known as "new age" or "new jazz." It has a smoother, contemporary sound, and the rhythm underlying the melody can make it quite exciting to hear and ride to. This style has become very popular for freestyles because it often has a steady beat, is usually played on synthesized instruments and can represent many moods. Some well-known musicians include Enya, Yanni, Mannheim Steamroller, John Tesh and Ottmar Leibert (to name just a few).

Ragtime

Ragtime is not quite like any other American style of music. Though it is considered jazz, it has a unique and distinct form all its own. It was considered to be at its height in the early part of the 20th Century and is most commonly heard in the music of Scott Joplin, whose music was used in the popular movie *The Sting* starring Paul Newman and Robert Redford.

In ragtime music the rhythm pattern accents are in unexpected places, which is very odd and electrifying. This is called "syncopated." Because ragtime music is basically piano music, the player's left hand keeps a regularly accented bass beat while the right hand decorates the tune with runs and syncopation. Written in 2/4 time with crisp enunciation, this type of music is especially suited for a horse in trot.

The march is one of the major sources of ragtime composition as found in titles such as "March and Two-Step," "Honolulu Ragtime Patrol," "March a la Ragtime," and many others with tempo indications ("tempo di Marcia") in their titles. Therefore, the rag and the march share common ground, providing music in 2/4 time. It is the rhythmic impulse of ragtime through its characteristic "swing" that has made its use popular for freestyles.

Big Band

This style of music can also be called "swing." It developed from forms of jazz that were popular during the 1930s. Principally played by groups called "big bands," it was very popular for dancing due to its upbeat sound and "catchy" melodies. This music brought a shift from the two-beat rhythm found in earlier styles to a rhythm in which all beats in a measure could receive comparable emphasis.

The bands, usually comprised of a mix of saxophones, trumpets, trombones, piano, double bass, guitar and drums, were typically led by well-known soloists such as Benny Goodman, Glenn Miller and Tommy Dorsey. Many times there were also vocalists who traveled with these bands.

Swing music has a strong, moving beat, ear-pleasing harmonies and a melody that lingers with you. The music became popular, as it was played over and over, and eventually produced "hit" songs. Many of these songs have never gone out of style and are now considered "standards" of the genre—songs such as "Stardust," "String of Pearls," "Chattanooga Choo-Choo," "Little Brown Jug," and many more. They have a strong appeal to many people and, because of the dance-like rhythm of the style, are wonderful to use for freestyles. While many of these songs do contain vocals, many more don't and it is also possible to find instrumental versions. Moreover, there is a huge repertoire to select from and most all have universal appeal that works wonderfully for freestyle.

Classical

Classical music is primarily a period of music identified as being from about 1770 to 1830. Popular composers from this time were Beethoven, Hayden and Mozart. This type of music is generally characterized by regular recurrence of short, clearly articulated phrases, often combined in symmetrical patterns.

Another style of music that is often "lumped" with the classical category is Baroque. This is music from a period dating from about 1600 to 1750 and includes such composers as Monteverdi, Frescobaldi, Bach and Handel.

Generally, types of music included within the classical style are symphonies, cantatas, operas, sonatas and waltzes. Some styles of classical may be light, such as Roccoco, Italian or French, while some others may be of a "heavier" sound, such as music from the composers Wagner and Beethoven.

A more recent composer whose work is often called "Modern American" but is also considered classical is Aaron Copeland. He was born in 1900 and was head of the composition department at the Berkshire Music Center at Tanglewood, New York, from 1940 to 1965. Among his better known works are "Appalachian Spring," "Rodeo," "Billy the Kid" and "Dance Panels".

Frequently, riders who are new to musical freestyles assume that because dressage is "classical," only classical music can be used. This is definitely not so! In fact, classical music may be the most difficult to use successfully due to its constantly changing tempos, "dead space" (long pauses with no sound) and often not enough measures of a useable section. Also, because there is such a vast repertoire of music to choose from, it could take quite a while to discover that special piece.

Movies and Musicals

Another style of music that is very popular for freestyles is music written for movies or musicals. This style of music can be very dramatic and is good because it presents the opportunity for a complete "theme" for the freestyle with music that can work with all the gaits.

Popular Music

Popular music is modern music that primarily comes from the second half of the twentieth century and includes rock, disco, country/western, bluegrass, Motown and pop. Many of these songs were hit vocals from groups such as The Beatles and are now available in instrumental forms. Many of these instrumental recordings have been performed by well-known orchestras such as the Boston Pops, the Cincinnati Pops or the Royal Philharmonic Orchestra.

Another type of modern music, though it uses both classical and modern pieces is the "Hooked-On" series of recordings. This style became popular in the 1980s when K-Tel put a synthetic beat, via synthesizer, on easily recognizable classics such as "Flight of the Bumblebee" or "A Fifth of Beethoven." While this particular type of music is very stylized and may become monotonous after a while, it is very good for a beginner freestyle because the beat is very clear and regular. This genre now includes an entire repertoire of music from classical to swing to marches.

Half-Time Music

You might also consider using half-time music, which means that the horse will be at half the tempo of the music. Or, put another way, the music is playing double-time—double the tempo of the horse. For example, let's assume we are using music that times at 120 beats per minute. The horse walks or passages at 60 beats per minute, so the heavy downbeat will fall only every other stride. The Queen's Guards in England parade at half-time, which is very regal but can be difficult for a beginner to use effectively. It takes a good ear and a sense of rhythm to follow this type of music.

Because each horse and rider combination is different, half time music is workable and comfortable for some riders while, for others, it is perturbing and overpowering.

Vocal Music

There has been much discussion regarding the use of vocal music in freestyles. The general consensus is that vocal music should not be used because it can be distracting from the overall ride. However, it is possible that some vocals can be used as accents within the choreography. Remember, however, that the person you are trying most to impress is the judge. If vocal music is distracting to the audience, it will also likely be so to the judge.

Fanfare Music

The last common style of music we'll discuss here is fanfare music. Fanfare music is music that has been written specifically to announce or draw attention to the beginning of an event. A well-known piece of fanfare music is the theme for 20th Century Fox movie studio that is used at the beginning of each film.

This style is great to use for your entrance because of the "Ta-da" aspect that it implies. Since you want the judge to sit up and take notice as you enter, a fanfare piece may be just the thing for the entrance to your freestyle.

There are many classical and swing pieces that start with a fanfare. There are also recordings of only fanfare music (mostly European). As this is music that is used as an attention-getter, you need not be concerned with beats per minute.

Sources for Music

Most of us have some sort of music collection at home—whether it is comprised of records, cassettes or CDs. Your first source of music should be what you have on hand. Music can be very costly if you plan on starting with an all-new collection. Look for music sources that won't cost you anything—or very little. Here are a few ideas:

- **Friends.** In addition to borrowing music from friends, you can exchange ideas on music.

- **Thrift Stores.** These can be a great source of music, especially of older music that may not be available at current music stores.

- **Libraries.** If you haven't been to the library for a while, you may be surprised at all the music possibilities available. You can check out as much music as you wish to search, and once you have identified music you like, you can go and make your purchase at the store.

- **_Flea Markets and Yard Sales._** Scour flea markets, yard sales, rummage sales and garage sales. You can often find an abundance of old standards. Keep your eyes open for boxes hidden under the sellers' tables.

- **_Radio Stations._** Listen, listen, and listen. When you hear something you think might be good but have missed the title, note the date and time and call the radio station. These stations usually maintain a "play list" of all music and they can look up the name of the piece that was playing at that time.

- **_Internet._** Another resource now available to the freestyle enthusiast is the Internet. One such Web site is Dressage UnLimited, located at dressage.com. This is an exciting Web site that covers many different aspects of dressage, including freestyles. For a fee, you can join and access, among other things, a music list that has been prepared by the site's freestyle host, Mike Matson. I have worked with Mike in the past, and he uses a cataloging method similar to what will be discussed in the next section. He keeps a current list of music possibilities complete with tempo notations and other comments. It's quite a list, and a lot of fun to read.

Listening To Music

Generally speaking, most people are apt to listen to music while doing something else—listening only enough to be merely aware of the music. Now that you are involved with designing a freestyle, you will have a new awareness of all the music that surrounds you. You need to take the time and opportunity, through active listening, to compare and analyze music in order to develop the ability to make good judgments about what can be used for your freestyle ride. As you become an *active listener,* you will be able to analyze music to the extent of hearing rhythm patterns, phrases, tempo, loud, soft, fast, slow, light, happy, etc. I find that I can no longer can just sit in a movie and enjoy the story—the music is always catching my ear, and I find myself asking, "Would this work for a freestyle?"

Practice timing music so that you can do it quickly if you hear music that sounds like it might work for you and your horse. The best way to practice determining tempo is to listen to recordings that you are familiar with, and time it as we discussed in Chapter 5. Not all music contains distinct patterns. Listen for the accent in the music or the strong downbeat. This is where you can tap your foot, clap your hands or jog in place to the beat.

This discovery method can be an exciting, stimulating and rewarding way to learn. Listening to music is really an adventure of discovery of musical sound and how you respond to it. How you respond will give you a good idea of how a judge and audience might respond later on.

Your Music Library

By analyzing your music collection, you'll make your own music library more functional. This information can be kept in a variety of ways, such as a notebook, a card file or on your computer.

The easiest method I've found to keep track of my music library is to first give each album, cassette or CD a unique number. I write down the number in a notebook and tag this number on the CD or album jacket. That way, all my albums are arranged in numerical order in the rack and, as you will see, this makes them easier to locate when you need them.

Record Number	Song Title	Time	Gait	Music Type	BPM
7	Lady	3:15	Trot	Cha Cha	
10	Love Makes the World Go Round	2:42	"	Dixie Waltz	
76	Oklahoma	2:50	"	Show Tune	
16	Figaro	2:12	"	Classic	
78	God Bless America	3:05	"	Patriotic - I. Berlin	

Record Library Card Sample

Once an album, cassette tape or CD is logged in, I listen to each of the songs it contains. First, I just listen. I mentally note which pieces seem to have the right sound. Do they have vocals? If yes, I usually mark NG—not good—next to them on the jacket and don't use them. Then I go back and begin to time each piece that seems suitable. Sometimes you may only have one usable piece on an entire album.

As I time each piece, I write the number of beats per minute next to the title on the jacket listing. That way it's noted on the album or CD itself. Then, in my notebook, I have set up separate pages for each beat per minute (50, 51, 52, 53, 54…78, 79, 80, 81, 82…98, 99, 100, 101, 102, etc.).

By the time I've listened to and categorized several recordings, I will have listed all music that is of a certain tempo under that tempo's heading. Then, when I go out in the arena and time that a horse is moving at 80 beats per minute, I can look at my 80 beats per minute page and see all the pieces that I have in my collection at that tempo. It makes the search for music at a given beat a lot easier.

Chapter 7

Adding the Choreography

Leigh Ann Hazel-Groux

*T*he magnitude of putting together a freestyle can be overwhelming for all riders—beginners and experienced alike. Regardless of riding experience or musical training, sometimes it's difficult to figure out where to start. However, you will reach the point where it all comes together, and the finished product will give you many hours of enjoyment during practice, competition or just "dancing with your horse." The key is having a plan that suits you and your horse.

By the time you begin thinking about choreography, you should know what level freestyle you will perform. If you are not sure, ask yourself what level you are currently training. While it is not a requirement, USDF recommends that you ride a freestyle one level below the one you are training. If you are having difficulty with the required movements of a certain level, putting them to music cannot camouflage those difficulties. Also, it can actually make the movement seem more difficult to ride.

Technical proficiency is an absolute that needs to be understood and achieved before riding a freestyle. As has been previously discussed, if you and your horse have not yet achieved competency at a given level, adding the challenge of working with and riding to music isn't wise. Mary Campbell was quick to say, "Good music and great choreography cannot make up for bad riding."

The Importance of Good Riding

There is such a concern regarding the technical correctness of the riding and training that in 2001, the USDF voted to require a minimum percentage that must be met before a rider may enter a freestyle competition. The current rule states that "In order to enter a freestyle class at any level, a horse/rider combination must have received a minimum score of 58% in the highest test of the declared freestyle level or any test of a higher level at a USAE Recognized Competition." While this requirement has met with some resistance from those who said it would discourage freestyle participation, its purpose cannot be overlooked—it ensures the correct training of the horse.

Once you have decided on the level, get a copy of the USDF freestyle test sheet at that level for the current year. These are available by contacting USDF (the address and phone number for the USDF are located in the Appendix at the back of this book). Once you get the test, read it thoroughly. You will notice that it gives you lots of information such as the compulsory movements, a list of what movements are allowed—as well as those that are clearly forbidden. The back of the test sheet lists useful tips in information to the judges regarding definitions, time limits, length of entrance music, opening and closing halts, etc.

Choreography Basics

Now that you know what your parameters are, begin by asking yourself what order you want to ride the gaits, for example,

1. walk, trot, canter;
2. trot, walk, canter, trot;
3. canter, walk, trot;
4. walk, canter, trot; etc.

Once you have this basic outline, you can begin to put the selections of the music for each gait in the order of gaits you have chosen, and edit their length to fit the approximate time it will take to complete all the required movements. The time limit for all USDF Freestyle tests is five minutes. That means you cannot go over that time without incurring a penalty that is two points deducted from the artistic impression. In addition, any movements performed after the five-minute limit will not be scored. This is important to remember when you are planning your music outline.

Planning Your Ride

Now that you have chosen your music, are acquainted with your test and its requirements, and have a basic outline of the order of gaits, you can begin to put together the plan for your ride. Here is a rough idea of the time it takes to perform the movements required for each gait (these numbers work best for tests at the lower USDF levels).

> **Trot:** 2 min. to 2 min. 20 sec.
> **Walk:** 30–45 sec.
> **Canter:** 1 min., 45 sec.

These times are approximate, but they will give you a starting point for editing your music selections to the necessary length. It is advisable not to have the combined times of the different gaits exactly match the time limit of the test. I usually recommend keeping it at least 5 seconds short of the time limit due to the fact that, especially when dealing with cassette tapes, different recorders can play back at slightly different speeds. While you may not be able to audibly detect this, if you are right at 5 minutes for instance, the judge's stopwatch may record you at 5 minutes, 5 seconds, thus incurring the penalties previously mentioned. On the other hand, if when you have finished choreographing your ride, it is four minutes, 40 seconds, don't feel compelled to make it a full five minutes. However, there is a note on the back of the freestyle test that suggests that rides shorter than four minutes and 30 seconds may also be subject to lower scores.

The FEI levels are different in regard to time limits. In the Prix St. Georges, Intermediaire I, Junior and Pony Rider tests, the maximum time is still five minutes, but there is also a minimum time of four minutes, 30 seconds. For the Grand Prix Freestyle, the maximum time is six minutes and the minimum time is five minutes, 30 seconds. This increase in time is to allow for the greater number of movements required at Grand Prix level.

In the Grand Prix Freestyle, a slightly different approach to choreography may be appropriate because of the additional movements of piaffe and passage. Again, you can map out the order of gaits as explained above and begin to put together a rough arrangement of your chosen music. You also need to consider your horse's physical and technical abilities, his strength to perform piaffe and passage, and how to arrange these movements to best show off your horse. A younger, less experienced horse may not be able to perform the piaffe and passage longer than about one minute, whereas an older, experienced Grand Prix horse may be able to sustain these movements for quite a bit longer. This needs to be taken into account when planning how long each section of the ride should be.

Moving to the Music

I like to go back to the music I've selected in order to develop the choreography, letting the phrasing and emphasis within the music suggest either where to begin or end movements, as well as suggesting movements themselves.

An example of Grand Prix "mapping" could be as follows:	
Passage/Piaffe	:45
Trot	1:12
Walk	:32
Canter	2:04
Trot	:24
Passage/Piaffe	:45
Total Ride Time	**5:42**

A horse performing this ride must have great strength and gaits to start with passage/piaffe (a glimpse of the most difficult movement), maintain the sparkle throughout the walk, trot and canter movements, and still be able to dazzle the judges and audience with the final passage/piaffe tour.

For example, if your music has a strong, emphatic phrase, this may be a good place for an extension or lengthening of the gait. If there is a more melodic flow to the music, it may be a good place for circles or serpentines at the lower levels, or some half pass or leg yield at the higher levels.

It is advisable to diagram your ride as you begin developing your choreography. A simple way to do this is to keep several sheets of paper on a clipboard with blank arenas drawn on them. As you put a pattern of movements together that work well, you can quickly draw them in. The advantages are several:

1. You'll remember what you did,

2. It helps you to see at a glance if you have included all the required movements shown in both directions and,

3. It lets you get a birds-eye view of the overall pattern and choreography and whether it is symmetrical and balanced.

It is important to use the entire arena—your "stage." Don't confine your ride to just one side of the arena or to the

Blank arenas for sketching ride ideas

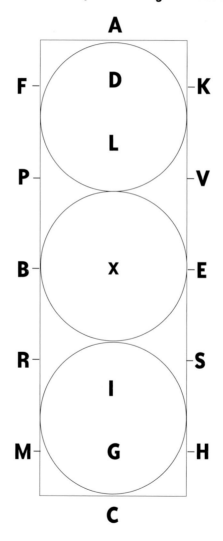

center. Use the entire arena—corners, quarter lines, center-lines, full diagonals, half diagonals. Also, as you think about your movements, plan not only where you wish to begin a movement but also where you will end it as you segue into your next movement.

As you add the choreography to your selected music, put yourself in the judge's seat and consider what your ride will look like from his or her perspective. This will help you become aware of what the judge can see and will help you decide how and where to place stronger (or weaker) movements to show them to the best advantage. Never try to fool the judges. They are always on the lookout for "cheating" moves such as the walk away from the judge, or extended movements shown only from behind. Be sure to use movements that will highlight your horse's strengths, not just hide weaknesses.

Once you have a good idea of the movements that you and your horse can do well and know how to show them off well to the judge, go ahead and note these things on paper so when you begin working with your music, you can refer to them. You might even put together a short choreography without music, such as a combination of required movements like half pass, extension, and serpentine/circles at a given gait such as the trot, making sure you have used all the required elements. Have a friend videotape or time it for you, and this way you will have a more accurate idea of how long the music selection should be. And, while watching the video, you can begin to determine if the choreography has a good flow or needs to be adjusted for clarity of a given movement or its placement in the ring. It also is a way for you to work with your horse on combinations that will help you determine which placement of movements could show him off to best advantage.

Make a Grand Entrance

Entrance music for a musical freestyle can be very dramatic and set the stage for your solo performance. The judge looks up, the audience looks up, and it captivates their eyes to watch the onstage musical freestyle performer—you.

Your choice of entrance music will do several things for you: First, you, the rider, will feel a stimulation that will set you in a dancing mood for the performance. Music stirs the emotions, produces a beat, rhythm and titillation that you can revel in. In addition, the audience is called to attention (the "Ta-da" factor) and subconsciously shares this feeling with you. Showmanship, the art of dressage, and music will captivate those that are in the listening and viewing realm.

The other practical task that entrance music performs is to assure that the sound system is on and working. Once when beginning a freestyle, I signaled for the music to start and waited. When my entrance music finally began, it was several seconds ahead of where it should have been. The music operator had not turned on the outside speakers before starting my tape! In this case, it turned out all right. We cantered very quickly and managed to arrive at our scheduled opening halt just in the nick of time and went on to have a spectacular ride.

Your entrance music does not count as part of your allotted ride time: The judging of your freestyle begins with your opening halt and ends with your final halt. However, the entrance music should have the same mood or tone as the music you have selected for your ride, but it is not necessary that the beats match your gaits exactly. Often, it is possible to find fanfare-type music that will match your theme, which can provide a very dramatic opening.

According to USAE rules, you must signal the sound operator within 60 seconds of the entry bell or whistle, and you have 20 seconds to enter the ring once your music begins. As you await the judge's signal, review your pre-entry checklist: Hands: Where are they and what are they doing? Feet and legs: Are they where you know they should be? Are you sitting correctly with nice posture? Are you smiling? Your confidence will shine through the entrance music and announce that a wonderful performance is about to take place.

The quickest way to find your starting point outside of the arena where you will commence with your entrance music is done like this: Halt at the spot where you plan to make your opening halt but face A, not C. Signal your helper to start your entrance music. When it starts, ride down the centerline out of the arena, turning either right or left at A, depending on the direction from which you prefer to enter the arena. Stop when your entrance music stops. Turn around and note where you are. This is where you need to position yourself before you signal the music operator to begin your music. Signal your helper to begin your entrance music again and, this time, ride into the arena. When the entrance music ends, you should at the place you want to salute the judge, but now facing C and ready to begin your ride.

Opening Moves

Open your freestyle with a movement you feel especially good about and one that your horse performs well. This will give you an attention getting opening, and you will have confidence that you can do this from the very beginning of your ride. Be confident in your strengths, use them to be inventive and show the movements that your horse performs well to their best advantage. While you cannot ride movements above the level, you may combine required

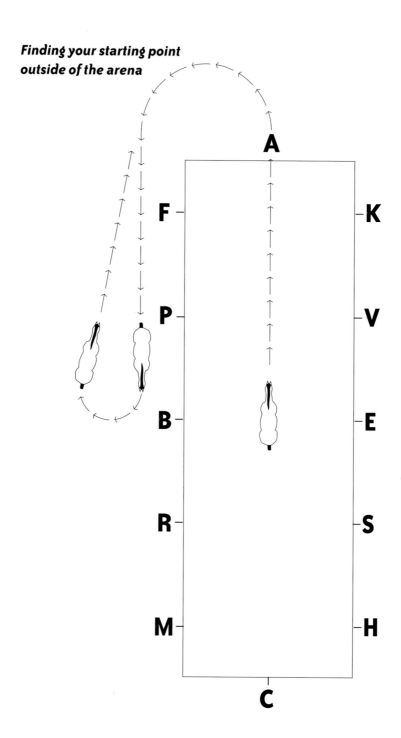

Finding your starting point outside of the arena

A

F — — K

P — — V

B — — E

R — — S

M — — H

C

104

movements in such a way that they may resemble those found in higher levels and yet still fall within the guidelines. Remember, a ride that resembles a compulsory test will not be considered creative or interesting. Again, refer to your test sheet for the list of movements, both allowed and forbidden. Also, if you have questions, ask. If you are not sure who would know, contact USDF for their suggestions, or if you are acquainted with a technical delegate or judge, they could help to clear up any confusion you may have.

Let's use the example of a client I worked with—a child competing at Training Level in Pony Club. The requirements for the level included 20-meter circles in trot and canter. While the child had difficulty keeping her pony cantering on straight lines, she could do canter circles very well. Therefore we planned the ride—and the music —so she only cantered on circles. The test might not have flowed as smoothly as it might have for a more experienced rider, but the requirements were met, and she received a good score on her circles. MORAL: Know yourself and your horse, show yourself off to your best advantage and don't "bite off more than you can chew" by attempting things beyond your level of ability.

The Middle

Once you've gotten started with a couple of good opening movements, again study the requirements as you begin to get a feel for the flow and directions your choreography is taking. Remember that the judge will be seated at C and it is good to orient movements in his/her direction. For example, half pass or leg yield toward the judge at least once. You can move away from the judge in your test as well, but it is good to give him or her a good look at what you and your horse do best. Also, judges are very aware of riders who try to disguise movements by performing them away from C (such as a free walk down the center toward A).

Again, listen to your music and try to use the phrases and emphases in the music to suggest choreography. A drum-roll or increase in volume at the beginning of a phrase can suggest an extension or lengthening, while if a melody or phrase repeats several times, that may be a good opportunity for a leg yield or half pass zig-zag. Also, you may perform movements more than once, especially if your horse does them well. A good use of this could be in planning your tempi changes. For instance, if you plan to do a couple of lines of three tempi changes and you also are required to do four tempi's and only plan one of those, if your horse misses on the four's, you could substitute one of the lines of three with another line of four.

Remember when planning your ride, try to avoid making it "test-like." Don't copy movements from the regular tests. Also, be sure to make use of the entire arena, don't have all your movements occurring on one side of the ring or the other. Keep it balanced with a feeling of symmetry. At the same time, take advantage of the arena and make use of quarter lines, short and three quarter-length diagonals, such as from F-E, E-M or F-S. All these are elements that work toward making your ride interesting and beautiful.

Go Out with a Bang

The last impression of a freestyle ride is as important as the first because it will color the judge's opinion of the entire performance.

When planning the end of your ride, make sure you have one! You want to make sure that both your music and your choreography arrive at the climax together. If you have a weak conclusion, you may leave both the audience and judge disappointed. A strong freestyle, for example, that has no definitive musical end such as strong chord accompanied by a dramatic halt but just "peters out," will leave an impression of incompleteness. Therefore, think of your ride as a three-act play, with an explosive beginning, a stimulating middle, and a strong ending.

An important note here: According to USDF rules, exit music is not regulated. However, under USAE and FEI Rules for freestyles, exit music is not allowed under penalty of elimination.

Perfecting Your Ride

Wow! You did it! You have chosen music, choreographed your ride and are ready to go! Or are you? Actually, you have just completed the first steps even though you feel as if you have been at it quite a long while. Now begins the work of polishing and perfecting your ride.

You may find that after you have worked all the movements through, put them together with your music and diagrammed it all out, that there are places that need "tweaking"—editing or adjusting. Don't be discouraged. This is the work that makes a freestyle truly great. As you refine your ride, focus on how it works together. Sometimes, this may mean re-editing parts of the music to make the phrasing work out timing-wise with the movements. Other times, you may need to alter your choreography with a change in gaits or within specific movements to better match the phrasing of the music.

Here again is an opportunity to use video to help you evaluate your ride. Have your helper video a total run-through while standing at C and watch it, keeping in mind the tips for freestyle judges found on the back of your test sheet. Ask yourself some of these questions: Does the choreography make full use of the arena with cohesiveness and creativity of design? Is the harmony between horse and rider clearly seen? Does the music highlight the horse and vice versa? Are the required movements clearly shown? You don't want to leave the judge guessing on this one.

Don't be afraid to make changes. If the basic design is good, sometimes a few simple changes will make it better. Also, make sure to get input from your instructor—if you haven't done so already. In addition, even after you've begun to perform your freestyle at shows, if a judge makes a comment that seems to make sense, use it. One of the freedoms of freestyle is that it is not a compulsory test and refinements may always be added.

Chapter 8

Recording Your Music

Leigh Ann Hazel-Groux

As we've discussed, there are many elements involved in putting together your freestyle plan. These involve choosing great music that has a theme, developing balanced choreography that includes a good beginning, a middle and a great ending.

In this chapter we will focus on making your music cassette tape or CD. Given all the technology that has been developed in the recording field over the last 10 years, this chapter will attempt to give an overview of what is available today rather than a step-by-step on the mechanics of "how to" for making your tape or CD.

Recording Options

There are a number of ways to have a cassette tape or CD made for your freestyle ride. The method you choose to use will depend on your time, available equipment and resources. Many riders are limited by time constraints such as family, full-time jobs or other responsibilities. Others may not have the music resources or the basic equipment needed for recording. They must have a tape or CD made for them by a professional.

There are several ways to produce your music tape or CD:

1. Learn about and use your own equipment.

2. Assemble your music selections, and make an appointment to work with a recording engineer at his or her studio.

3. Hire a professional to make your entire tape or CD using the music you selected.

4. Work with studio musicians to make an original recording of music specifically designed for your freestyle.

Cassette or CD?

As you begin to work on your music, you need to decide whether to use a cassette tape or a CD to record your music. Cassette tapes and CDs essentially have the same ability to record music, however, how this happens is different in each case. Cassettes consist of a plastic tape coated with a ferromagnetic material, which means that if it is exposed to a magnetic field (the tape recorder), it is permanently magnetized until the information is recorded over. In contrast, CDs produce their sound digitally, which makes the sound clearer and sharper—the recording is closer to the original than if it were recorded on a tape. Another difference lies in the longevity—CDs hold up better while cassettes can wear out and even break.

Very often the CD versus cassette decision ultimately depends on the nature of the competition—whether it is international, national, regional, local or schooling—and the type of music-playing equipment the show grounds use. Some shows, particularly at the schooling-show level and local show grounds, may only possess cassette players as their show sound system. The show's prize list will often specify what medium is preferred, but if you should have a question, contact the show secretary to ask.

Now, let's take a closer look at these recording mediums and how to use each to achieve the best playback quality.

Cassette Tape

The cassette tape is the most common medium for use in home recording at the present time. However, with the advancement in home recording on the computer via CD technology, this will most likely not be the case for long.

Cassette tapes are also known as "analog tapes." Analog recording systems record sound in a manner "analogous" to the original pattern (a continuously varying waveform). This simply means that the recording corresponds to the original.

If you decide to use a cassette, for best home results, start with a new, high-quality, low-noise, 30-minute tape. Consider these key cassette tape features:

- compatible with virtually all cassette decks
- low noise and high output
- good overall sound quality and reliability.

The quality of and type of tape used has a lot to do with the capabilities of your equipment, so you should use the right type for your particular recording needs. When you purchase a cassette package, it will have an audiocassette selector guide to choose from. There are three types: Type I—Normal, Type II—CrO2 (chrome) and Type III—Metal. Although Type III cassettes provide excellent music reproduction, they must be recorded and played on machines that have the correct settings and may sound distorted when played on a Type I machine.

Therefore the most appropriate tape to use for freestyle music recordings is a good quality Type I cassette as it can be played on any equipment—a very important consideration. Be sure to use a recognized brand tape as some cheaper varieties use poor quality materials and will not last very long.

CDs

CD (compact disc) technology has been available since the early 1980s, but it has come into its own during the last decade. Most every home now has a CD player, as do most automobiles. CDs are also very accessible as a recording medium on computers. All you need is a CD burner, a software program and a little understanding of how it all works.

CDs produce music recordings through a digital process that produces a clear and accurate reproduction of sound. Digital audio systems record by breaking up the continuity of the sound in to smaller values known as "samples." It is these samples that enable the analog sound to be converted to digital signals, which can be read by the computer and subsequently recorded onto the disc.

There are multiple programs available on the market today that can be used with your computer to produce CDs. While at one time Macintosh computers were the acknowledged leaders in the computer field for music software, there are now many software programs that work well for PC technology also.

DAT

Another recording medium that can be used is Digital Audio Tape (DAT). DAT is a digital recording system that takes analog sound, converts it into a digital format and records it onto special cassettes as a digital code, thus avoiding the problems of "tape hiss" inherent in analog tape recordings. DAT tapes can only be recorded and played on DAT machines and are often used for "master" tapes. However, this type of recording is not widely available except in professional studios and while could be used for a "master" recording, the final would still need to be produced on tape or CD.

Preparing Your Practice Tape

Once you have selected your music and have begun to work on your choreography, you want to record your practice tape so it's as close to the finished product as possible. Remember: This is not a one-step process that will be completed perfectly on the first attempt. Think of this as a preliminary step, which will be refined and polished into the final version—whether you produce the final yourself or go to a studio professional.

If you have put your music in "gait order" as was discussed in Chapter 7, you are already on your way. The next step is to organize and edit the sections of music into the correct lengths of time needed for each gait.

Begin with your entrance music. Remember, only 20 seconds are allowed for your actual entrance to the halt/salute beginning your ride. When you record this onto a tape, give yourself a little lead-time on the tape before beginning the music itself. On each cassette tape, there is a short amount of blank tape that runs before the actual recording section of tape begins. If you rewind the tape completely, and immediately begin to record from there, you will lose the first couple of seconds of music before the tape truly begins recording. After the entrance, I like to give a short pause of about three to four seconds for the opening halt and salute. Occasionally you can find a piece of music with an introduction of the correct length and build a pause into it before it begins on the main melody.

After the entrance and salute, your music should begin for the first gait in the choreography, which, in this example, is the trot. As we discussed in Chapter 7, the trot section will be approximately two minutes in length in a lower level freestyle. According to the plan, the trot is followed by 30–45 seconds of walk. Next comes the canter section that continues for approximately one minute, 45 seconds. Finally, you may have another 20–30 seconds of trot music leading up to your final halt and salute.

As you make your initial practice tape, this is where the concept of musical phrases comes in and your listening ability is put into practice. To recap, a musical phrase is a short musical thought—at least two, but typically four measures in length. (Remember the illustration from Chapter 4 of "Mary had a Little Lamb"?) The phrase is a natural division of the melody, and the length of time for one phrase will generally measure the same for each repetition of the phrase throughout the music. While you may not recognize the phrases at first, as you listen to the music and become familiar with it, listen for the natural pauses—think of them as "commas"—in the melody. If you measure 15 seconds for one phrase for instance, and need 30 seconds of music to ride to, you need to record two phrases.

For best results, don't end the music in the middle of a phrase, even if you are a bit short of or longer than the needed time. Recording until the end of a phrase will help to prevent abruptness in the music and keep it flowing. After you have made this initial tape and ridden to it, it will be an easy matter to adjust the ride or edit the tape to make it all work.

As you are recording your chosen music, make use of the counter on your tape recorder or CD player. This counter will show the time elasped in minutes and seconds of a given piece of music. If your player doesn't have such a counter, you can also use a stopwatch. Simply begin timing with the stopwatch at the start of the song and let it run through the entire piece. If you are not going to start recording at the beginning of a certain song, make a note where the counter is when you wish to begin recording, and also especially where you want to end a piece. This will make future revisions or recordings easier as you will know your starting and stopping points. Keeping track of what you are recording and how is critical to success, especially if you intend to take your music to a studio professional to record the final product.

If you are using the cassette deck of a component stereo system, you can use the "fade" control at the end of each piece to enable smoother transitions from one section of your music into another. If you are using a computer to do this, the software programs have built-in "fade out" and "fade in" controls which make blending sections quite easy.

Once you have made this first recording, it's time to take it out to the barn. Remember you are still in the early stages of the process and, again, realize that you will likely need to re-edit your tape, to add or shorten sections. You may also need to refine your choreography to better fit the music—especially if you designed your ride before you began working with the music. The key to getting through this process is to be patient. You may have to go back and forth several times between the riding and recording before arriving at the final freestyle recording.

Using a Recording Studio

Once you have basically completed work on your music and choreography, you may wish to take your tape and the timed segments of your ride to a recording studio for a more professional finish for your final tape or CD. To find a business that specializes in the services you need, look in your area Yellow Pages under Recording Studios.

In addition, there are now many businesses that specialize in designing dressage freestyles. Many advertise in the classified sections of horse magazines or on the Internet. These freestyle professionals offer many services from recording your final tape to choreographing your ride. Some even offer customized music recorded specifically for you and your horse.

Recording studios typically charge an hourly rate (this can range from $50 or more), which includes an engineer and the use of all studio equipment. Some businesses offer discounts for reserving block time, such as a four-hour minimum. Separate rates also may apply for studio musicians, if used, for arranging, performing and programming. Freestyle designers typically charge a set fee, which includes specific services such as tape or CD production, choreography and/or additional editing. Such fees can range from a few hundred dollars for a lower level ride to several thousand for an Olympic-level ride.

Tempo Changes

Changing the tempo of musical pieces (decreasing or increasing the speed of the music to match your horse's footfalls) can be done, but it should only be attempted with a good computer program or left to the expert in the studio. The reason is that when changes are made to the tempo, the pitch also changes, which can give an undesirable audio effect. Most modern computer editing programs can change tempo without changing pitch, but be careful not to overdo it, as there will be a noticeable loss of quality if it's pushed too far.

To understand what a change in pitch means, consider the recording of "The Chipmunk Song," popular at Christmas, or what playing a vinyl record at the wrong speed (such as a 33 1/3 record played at 78) sounds like. This makes the music faster, but it also alters the pitch of the music to a comedic point, making it sound higher and faster (like the Munchkins in the "Wizard of Oz") which can inspire laughter rather that awe.

If you find a piece of music that you feel you absolutely must use and its tempo needs altering, don't attempt to change it beyond 8–10 beats up or down or it will sound noticeably altered. If this is the case, your best option is to have it adjusted by someone who has the correct equipment to balance the tone and sound.

Copyright Issues

While copyrights for music used in freestyles is a subject that has brought about a tremendous amount of discussion over the years, you should be aware that all music is subject to copyright laws, except that which is considered public domain. Basically, any music written by an American author that pre-dates 1922 is considered to be in the Public Domain and may be freely used without permission. Otherwise, you should attempt to obtain permission from the owner of the copyright to use their music. A good Web site that provides information on this is www.pdinfo.com.

With regard to copyrights, USDF Freestyle Guideline 9 states: *According to Section 115 of the Copyright Act, a mechanical license must be obtained for the re-recording of music in any format. For information regarding obtaining a mechanical license it is recommended that the rider contact the National Music Publisher's Association, Inc., e-mail/Internet access — www.nmpa.org.*

USAE has recently reached an agreement with the American Society of Composers, Authors and Publishers (ASCAP) and Broadcast Music, Inc. (BMI) to "license music played in connection with competition at all USAE recognized and endorsed competitions and events held in the United States." This agreement became effective July 1, 2001, and "covers the playing of music that is copyrighted by ASCAP or BMI at USAE recognized competitions." A compete copy of the agreement can be obtained by contacting USAE at (859) 259-2472 or visiting the Web site www.equestrian.com. If you have any further questions concerning this, contact USDF or USAE for clarification.

Additional Tips

One problem inherent to using cassette tapes is that they can be accidentally erased. To minimize this from happening, once you are completely satisfied with the ride and tape, break out the safety tabs, or non-erase clips on the tape so it cannot be accidentally erased. These are small square clips on the narrow label end of the tape. Each side has its own tab. This will prevent you from losing all of the time and work you have invested.

You should make three finished tapes or CDs—two for showing and one for practice. Always give two copies of your music (the main tape and one as a backup in case of mechanical failure) to the show secretary with directions attached for the sound engineer (e.g., "I will signal you to start my tape when I position myself at the letter K"). If you have tapes just for show, keep them in your show trunk, that way you will always have them when you arrive at the show. Just remember if your trunk will be kept in the hot sun, you may wish to remove to tapes to a cooler location—tapes and heat don't mix. Keep your practice tape for working with at home. But remember, if you revise your tape at home, don't forget to replace the tapes in your show trunk as well.

If you are going to use a boom box for recording or to play for use at a schooling show, it is advisable to replace the batteries just before the show in case no electricity is available. Besides being assured of full power to the box, you will also take solace in knowing your batteries won't run out mid-ride.

Remember, once you have produced your finished tape, don't figure on it being the "absolute" final. There is always room and opportunity for refinement of your ride. Most times, these refinements will not result in a need to revise your music. However, sometimes after a show, there may be an area that must be fixed. If this happens, don't panic. It's all part of the process. The main thing is to enjoy it.

Sound Systems

Now you have your music and are ready to ride, but how should you listen to it? What is the best option? There are several different systems available to the rider. Each depends on where you will be listening to it and how much you wish to invest in a system for your own home use.

Boom Box

The first and most obvious choice is the boom box. This is a stereo cassette/CD player that is very portable and can be plugged in to an outlet or run on batteries. They come in many sizes, and there is a large selection available on the market.

Ideally, your boom box should have two large speakers which should be four inches in diameter or larger, a carrying handle, a good bass (for emphasis) and a pause control. Additional features available are dual cassette decks (useful for making copies of your tape), a digital tape/CD counter, capability to record and the ability to connect to other devices such as to your computer or to receive input from another source. If possible, when looking for such a box, play it at volume to hear its sound quality. Remember, if you are going to be using it at your ring, you need to be able to have the volume turned up enough to hear your music over the entire arena without sound distortion.

A good recommendation is the large Bose acoustic wave machine. This is not an inexpensive investment, but well worth it. The only drawback is that it is only available in a radio/CD format and is no longer available with a cassette tape player. You can check with your local Bose dealer to see what current technology is available.

The major disadvantage to the boom box is that you cannot ride with it attached to your saddle pad. Therefore, to use it in your arena, you either need to find a way to mount it, such as on a platform next to the ring at horse height so you can reach the controls or have a friend help you. And remember, having a friend can also be advantageous in terms of giving you feedback on how the ride looks as you practice it.

Portable Players

Another type of equipment popular today is the portable or personal cassette/CD player, sometimes called a "Walkman." This is a device that comes in a small size plays through headphones, rather that speakers. It is often used by people during exercising such as going to the gym, walking or jogging, but it can also be used while riding. The main thing is to make sure that you purchase one with anti-skip features and that you can attach it securely to yourself so it doesn't become dislodged in the middle of your extended trot.

There is also a device called Kur-Tunes, which consists of a nylon waist pouch that attaches like a belt. It has two small speakers and convenient volume controls for easy access. It is designed to work with your personal cassette player and weighs only eight ounces. Another option is a dressage saddle pad called Tunes to Go, made for the same purpose. Pockets behind the saddle flap on both sides hold amplified speakers, while another pocket behind the saddle holds a tape player.

Arena Systems

Obviously, the best solution for the serious freestyle rider is to install a sound system in the arena with controls at rider level. This offers several advantages such as not needing to remember to bring a boom box each time you want to work on your freestyle. Also, with a permanently installed system you can purchase speakers and performance decks that will give you maximum sound quality, which will help in determining the overall presentation of your music.

While most folks may not think a quality practice system would be of importance, keep in mind you want to hear and ride to the best sound you can for your freestyle. If you have an inadequate system, for example, if it vibrates at high volume or you can't get the volume high enough to hear it when you are riding, or it sounds "muddy" or muffled, you could miss nuances in the music that could highlight moments in your choreography. In addition, it allows you to hear any imperfections that may exist in your recording, hence giving you time to fix them before taking your ride to competition.

Should you desire to go the extra cost, Mike Matson, freestyle co-host of dressageunltd.com, has done considerable research on this topic and offers the following advice on purchasing a sound system for your arena:

Stereo Receiver: In a two-speaker system, 50–60 watts per channel at eight ohms is desirable and 80–100 watts per channel is even better. This is especially true if you listen to music at loud volumes, music with a loud bass, or use the system in a very large space such as a full-sized arena. To control distortion, look for a THD (Total Harmonic Distortion) specification of 0.1 percent or lower. You also want to have a loudness contour and Digital Sound Processing (DSP). The DSP feature allows the music to be reproduced so that it sounds like you are listening to it live in a concert-hall-type setting. Look for Dolby Pro Logic Surround, THX or Dolby AC-3. You also want to make sure your receiver and performance decks have a remote control—a required piece of equipment when operating from horseback.

Cassette Deck: When purchasing a cassette deck, two heads are adequate, and two or three motors are desirable. These motors drive the tape hubs forward and back for fast-forward as well as for rewind. Make sure the deck contains bias control, which ensures that the deck matches a particular type of tape, otherwise you can have problems with distortion and accuracy of playback. You also want to have noise reduction such as Dolby B (minimum), Dolby C (preferred), Dolby S (best) or Dolby HX Pro (a highly desirable feature). Without adequate noise reduction, an audible hiss will be present on all your recordings. As in the discussion on cassette tapes, it is important that the playback machine has the same or compatible type of noise reduction facility as the machine on which the tape was initially recorded.

Other features of convenience on a cassette deck include a double deck (useful for copying), a real time digital counter (counts in actual time elapsed, not an arbitrary counter number), repeat and memory rewind.

Note: Cleaning and lubrication are essential to the longevity and fidelity of a cassette deck, especially in an outdoor or dusty arena. Dirt and electronics don't always make a good mix and dirty players after a while either don't play very well, or don't play at all. Clean the heads every few hours of use and consider a periodic internal calibration, lubrication and cleaning done at the service shop.

CD Player: Buy a multi-disc CD player. This way if you are working with several CD's, you don't have to keep stopping to change them. There are two systems of loading discs into a multi-disc CD player—carousel or magazine. The carousel system is easier to use, more flexible and somewhat more reliable than the magazine. The CD player should have programming features that allow you to select which discs and tracks you want to play and in the order you want. It should also have a repeat feature allowing you to replay your programming.

Lungeing to music will be invaluable to developing your seat.
Heidi Graham and Olympus.

your horse's basic gaits. This security will allow you to be able to sit quietly and influence your horse with more sensitive and discrete aids. The art of riding is to make it appear effortless and beautiful so that the unskilled observer is unable to see how you manage to influence your horse without obvious signals and aids.

The easiest gait to start with while lungeing or being lunged is the trot because it has a clear, two-beat rhythm. Using the inside front left leg as your guide, make sure the horse maintains the one-two rhythm of the trot. As you are being lunged, ask yourself if you and your horse are both in time? You are the director of the tempo, so if the horse's tempo changes—speeding up or slowing down—you will need to correct it in order to match the tempo of the music.

Lungeing also can help to emphasize the importance of impulsion. It is essential not to confuse impulsion with simply speeding up. This becomes very clear when being lunged to music. Lively impulsion must be maintained from behind through a swinging back as the horse consistently moves forward into a steady connection. Playing music while lungeing the horse can be a tremendous help in establishing that your horse is moving forward with lively impulsion. If you selected music with the correct beats per minute for your horse, you will be able to tell immediately if the impulsion is off, because the gait and the music will not match.

The walk can also be improved with lunge work to music, both with and without the rider. The walk itself has little natural impulsion, but it will become more animated and improved as you encourage the four-beat sequence with suitable music. Again, use the horse's front inside leg as your guide. Music in 4/4 time will be correct and work well. In addition, lungeing over caveletti to music will help highlight the regular four-beat rhythm of the walk. Once the horse is comfortable and relaxed in the walk on the lunge, these qualities will hold over to work at the walk in the arena.

The canter work can be developed in the same fashion. Start by lungeing only the horse. Once the correct rhythm is established, the rider can be added. As you listen to the canter music, watch the horse's inside foreleg and count the three beats: 1-2-3, 1-2-3. The first beat will always be the leading foreleg.

Lungeing the rider to canter music will give her a great feeling of jump and will help mark the moment of suspension between the beats. Many riders tend to cling with their knees and thighs once the horse starts to canter. This is very restricting for the horse, who will respond by slowing down and losing the crisp jump. The horse may even fall into a trot. A rider must learn to relax and improve her position, sitting balanced on a three-point seat. Legs must hang down freely with loose, open thighs, allowing the horse unrestricted canter movement. Lungeing can give the rider balance, still hands and a secure seat, which will allow her to really ride a lovely, energetic canter forward into the bridle.

Music for Recreational Riding

There are many good books available that recite the theory and philosophy of the basic training principles required to school a horse and to create a happy and pleasant companion under saddle. These books also assist the rider in how to obtain the correct seat, body position, legs and hands in order to assist the horse in carry out the basic commands. Unfortunately, no matter how good the book, it is very difficult for an individual to interpret the correct rider position on a horse just by reading about it. Even with a good trainer it takes a long time for the beginner to look relaxed while sitting tall with legs hanging, hands steady and seat secure. This is the ideal picture we all have in our mind's eye, but it is so hard to achieve! Often the harder we strive to achieve the all-elusive secure seat with no "water skiing" on the reins for balance, the more tight and contorted our reluctant body becomes.

Before she can be a good dance partner for her horse, the rider must learn how to control her body. This is no easy feat. Some people are more coordinated than others, some have a better feel for rhythm, some are not shaped to look elegant on a horse, while others need to overcome a basic fear before they can relax and trust the horse.

One way to relax your body and feel the horse is to listen to and enjoy music while riding. Start by playing any music that you enjoy. It takes a little time to get used to riding to music if you are not used to it. Often you are so concerned with your horse and your body position that it is hard to listen well. Just take your time and relax. There is no hurry to achieve anything. I remember a quote from former Spanish Riding School Chief Rider Franz Mairinger: "Hurry slow."

You will find that riding to music during your riding sessions is self-rewarding. Horses often develop an excellent feel for music and will start to trot when the music changes to a two-beat rhythm and will voluntarily walk once the music changes to a four-time march. This helps you learn about beat, rhythm and tempo as you become more aware of the horse's rhythm. It will also remind you that he is not a passive partner in this musical enterprise.

Riding to music also makes you more aware of the space between you and your horse and the space around you and your horse. You realize that you have the time to relax, to think about your body while still being aware of your horse and the music. Suddenly tension, haste and frustration fade as you start riding in a new, relaxed way.

Music for Schooling

While similar to riding to music for recreation, the degree of sophistication increases as we become more particular when interpreting the music and striving to maintain an even rhythm. Much depends on your understanding of the basic movements and the correctness of your schooling.

Once you are relaxed, confident and have achieved a more correct position in the saddle, and the horse is in a better frame and is carrying himself in good balance, the music can be used to improve and develop the quality of the horse's gaits.

At this stage you will need help from a good trainer, ground person (friends or fellow riders), videotape or mirrors. Do not feel that you should be able to achieve your goals by yourself. All athletes need help to train and develop. Riders and potential freestyle participants are no exception.

Let's start with the walk, which, as we know, is a gait with a four-beat rhythm. Marches are common music choices for this gait, however, all types of music have sections with four beats and a nice walk feeling. Some pieces may prove just right for your horse. Once you have found the right music you can work with it while schooling the walk. Often, a horse with an unclear walk—one that is hurried, not regular or is lateral—can be helped significantly by riding to good, clear, four-beat music.

Music is great for exercises such as walk pirouette preparation. Ten-meter walk circles in travers become simpler when ridden to music because you are able to maintain the walk clarity. Later, with turn on the haunches and walk pirouettes, the clear beat of the walk music helps you to maintain a good walk while you complete the movement.

Music is just as helpful to the dressage rider at the trot as it is in the walk. The trot has fewer rhythm problems than the walk as it has only two diagonal beats, and the rhythm is a clear up and down. Many problems at the trot are related to speed. "Hurry and quick" is the message that some horses are given with the good intention of riding forward. Forward does *not* mean speed. Choose music with a clear beat that suits your horse's natural two-beat trot rhythm. Practice riding to this in the working trot on straight lines and through circles and turns. Practice until you can move all around the arena in the trot at the same rhythm. This is more difficult that it appears to be, but practice makes perfect. Once this goal is achieved you will feel more confident riding to the same rhythm.

Next you need to be able to shorten or lengthen the trot stride without disturbing the rhythm or tempo. Just to review, tempo is the rate of repetition of the rhythm. As the horse lengthens the trot stride, he must take longer steps but not increase the speed. A steady, even tempo is necessary to preserve the rhythmical swing of the horse. With the help of suitable music, you will learn to maintain an even and fluid trot through lengthening and collection.

Next on the schooling-to-music agenda is the ability to maintain the tempo during lateral exercises. Development of correct bending and maintenance of the outside rein throughout these movements is an essential element of the training scale. Again, having a ground person or using a videotape or arena mirrors can assist to guide you in this training. The music will be your friend, maintaining an even beat in two-time while you are struggling with the technical aspects the movement. As the shoulder-ins, travers and renvers become fluent, you will be able to move between these movements seemingly without effort. This happens when the rhythm of the music is secure in your mind, seat and heart.

The canter is a three-beat rolling gait with a moment of suspension. All styles of music have wonderful tunes for the canter beat. The canter rhythm evokes a strong feeling of power, fluidity of motion and regular beat with a moment of suspension to add an airborne moment unique to the gaits of the horse. The canter expresses the feelings and heart of the horse in motion. To a degree, the canter defines the horse himself.

Every horse has a different expression in the canter, and the right choice of music can highlight the beauty of the canter. Just riding to good, clear canter music will help correct problems in the canter itself. Horses that show a four-beat canter tendency or even a lateral canter can show immediate improvement by just riding forward to clear, three-beat music. Practice cantering around the arena on straight lines and on circles. Lengthening and half halts can become secure in a three-beat rhythm.

Riding, lungeing and schooling to music can be some of the most rewarding experiences in your equestrian career. This is without ever putting together a musical freestyle or attempting to choreograph movements to develop the musical story. Once you try experiment with schooling to music, you will never regret the decision. Both your riding and the basic gaits of your horse will improve dramatically as you learn to relax and ride freely forward to a regular rhythm. Try it and you'll enjoy the benefits.

Chapter 10

Development of the Quadrille, the Pas de Deux and Exhibition Riding

Libby Anderson

A Brief History

Though performing in freestyles in competition is fairly recent, the idea of them is not new. Exhibitions starring horses and riders performing spectacular patterns and movements have been held for centuries. They have been used to entertain the citizens of towns and countries, for circus, ballet, tournaments, holidays and celebration of victories on the battlefield.

Any number of horses and riders could be used depending on the size and style of the celebration. These rides could be performed by a single pair of horses and riders (pas de deux), to a quadrille of four horses and riders, or larger groups of eight, 12, 16 or 24 horses and riders. Even larger horse ballets were performed. These were extravaganzas, with beautifully costumed horses and riders, accompanied by actors, vocalists, musicians, stage scenery and especially composed music for the spectacular performance. Louis XIV of France celebrated one of the largest of these horse ballets in 1662. Such a grand spectacular of choreography, music and training of riders and horses could only be justified as a celebration of influence and power. In Vienna, Austria horse ballets were unequalled in finesse, beauty and cost. These exhibitions were unequalled anywhere else in the world. Unfortunately, as the popularity of the Baroque dwindled, the wonderful horse ballets faded into obscurity.

Later, in the eighteenth and nineteenth centuries, mounted Carousels became popular and carried on this entertainment on a smaller scale to the traditions of the horse ballet. The Spanish Riding School in Vienna, Austria, Saumur, France, The Andalusian School of Equestrian Art in Jerez de la Frontera, Spain and the Portuguese Escola de Equitaco in Alcainca, Portugal all carry the Baroque tradition of classical exhibitions, quadrilles and pas de deux to current times. These wonderful institutions have been a powerful voice for the horse and have brought classical equestrian through to the twenty-first century. Thus the historical heritage of riding to music has been preserved over the centuries through the many difficult years of motorization, industrialization, computer development and the Internet culture. All of this progress of civilization occurred between two bitter world wars and much international strife. Now, in the twenty-first century, the future of the horse is secure. Riding horses to music in competition has finally been established and recognized both by the national equestrian federations and the governing international body—the FEI.

Quadrilles

From fabulous exhibitions of quadrilles all over the world in the twentieth century there developed a serious interest in quadrilles for competition both in Europe, Great Britain and the USA. At the moment there is a serious possibility that the quadrille will be accepted by the FEI for Grand Prix competition. At present, the various national equestrian federations have promoted the quadrille as a legitimate form of equestrian competition. This is an exciting development as the quadrille offers the dressage enthusiast so many opportunities to enjoy and celebrate their sport. This includes team participation that is goal-orientated, and

A beautifully turned out quadrille team. Fresian Quadrille, Dressage at Devonwood, Portland, Oregon 2000.

Photo By: Terri Miller

the opportunity to develop musical creativity and expression which can make your particular quadrille special and memorable. And, quadrille participation is lots of fun and will definitely improve your basic riding skills.

In the United States the quadrille is alive and well thanks to the dedicated efforts of individuals, such as Californians Liz Searle and Jeff Moore over the past decade, and the acceptance of their ideas and innovations by the USDF and USAE. Quadrilles have gained acceptance in the dressage community and the Pony Club movement in the US with the result that riders are telling show management and organizers that they want to ride the official USDF approved quadrilles at the various levels in competition. By 2002 the quadrille had spread all over the USA in USDF recognized competitions. This is an exciting phase of development and will eventually expand to regional and national finals all over the USA.

To organize a quadrille, contact the USDF for a copy of the quadrille tests and rules and regulations. If you wish to compete, you need to be a participating member through your local riding or dressage club which is already affiliated or you can be an individual member of the USDF. You can also contact the USDF to find out if you are lucky enough to have such an association in your area. If not, your group can become innovators and pioneers and start up a quadrille association associated with your dressage chapter or region.

Besides being fun to do, riding quadrilles offers many benefits to riders. Stiff riders tend to relax as they concentrate on other things such as their alignment and synchrony while executing the movements. They feel more at one with the horse, more in control, more relaxed, sit more upright, hands are quieter and more supple, and most importantly, their minds are at peace.

Quadrilles require riders to execute movements at the

same time or with very specific timing. To do this, a horse must be on the aids and in front of the leg. As you begin to ride more proficiently, you will notice an improvement in your horse. The sluggish horse becomes more willing and forward, while the "hotter" variety responds to the half halts and becomes a more mellow citizen. Overall, the benefits of riding in a choreographed group are significant. You will make many friends while both you and your horse improve together to become a better-controlled dressage unit.

Quadrille Tests

Quadrilles are fun to watch, fun to ride and fun to judge. Just as the musical freestyle has become a dynamic and spectator friendly part of the national dressage community, so our "late bloomer"—the musical quadrille—is another good way to make dressage more accessible to the average dressage enthusiast and enables riding teams to compete for coveted awards.

The USDF offers various levels of tests for the quadrille. These levels correspond to the level of dressage that the prospective group of quadrille competitors is currently working. The levels follow the general principle for the current USDF and USAE dressage tests, which is that they are progressive through the levels.

Quadrille tests start with the Introductory level, which is the same level as the USDF Introductory dressage tests. This is a comfortable level for new quadrille participants to enter competition because it is only performed at walk and trot in a 20 by 40 meter arena. Horse and rider may be at a solid at Training level in traditional dressage tests, however it is a different matter to coordinate four horses and riders in a small arena without any problems. Remember, "Hurry slow." Once you read the Introductory Level tests you may realize that you need to bone up on some of the commonly used commands and definitions. Also, the collective marks read a little like a science fiction book: Spacing, Synchrony and Alignment!

Quadrille Terms

We need to define and discuss the basic requirements to take the science fiction out of the collective marks. To do this we will discuss all the commands and instructions for all the quadrille tests from Introductory to Second Level. For your convenience copies of all the USDF quadrille tests are printed in the appendix at the back of this book. Commands in the tests must be clear and concise so that the entire group understands the movements required. The following list is taken from *Primer for Judging the Quadrille*, by Sandy Howard, Jane Escola and Kathleen Wyland, published in 2002 by the California Quadrille Association.

Alignment

Alignment occurs in two directions: in a column (file) or laterally:

Column alignment: Whether in single file or in pairs, this refers mainly to centerline work. Alignment should be such that the judge at C can see only the first rider or riders if in pairs.

Lateral Alignment: Mainly seen when riders turn individually from the long side and go across the arena. The judge at C should be able to see only the nearest rider when alignment is correct. It is the riders' bodies that are aligned, not the horses' heads.

Cloverleaf

A figure formed when riders are coming in pairs from opposite directions on the centerline, and at the quarter markers (10 meters from each end of the arena) perform individual 10- meter circles, making the E-B line the center between the circles.

Column or File

Used interchangeably to describe riding one behind the other. This can be either single-file or double-file (in pairs).

Fan Formation

When coming down the centerline in pairs for a salute, the second pair splits and the riders fan out to come up alongside of the center pair.

Impulsion

Degree of forward energy. Judged as to whether or not it is adequate for the level being ridden.

Lateral Quarter Line

This is the line that transverses the arena from quarter-marker to quarter-marker.

Oblique

Refers to an angular line of travel from the centerline to the rail or from the rail to the centerline or opposite side of the arena, as opposed to straight across.

Pass Through

Refers to pairs approaching each other, making sufficient room to allow one horse to pass between the approaching two horses.

Quarter Marker

A point located ten meters from the corner of the arena (one quarter of the arena.)

Spacing

There are two kinds of spacing: column and lateral.

Column Spacing refers to distance between riders when riding single file, or pairs when riding in a column. Exact distance is not specified—experienced teams can use nose to tail spacing while beginning teams may prefer more distance. It is essential that the spacing be uniform for each movement. Spacing may be changed from movement to movement, depending the gait or the pattern.

Lateral Spacing refers to the spacing between two or more riders when approaching the judge head-on, such as in the salute. It would also apply in individual turns across the arena, but not easily seen by the judge at C.

Submission

Refers to the connection over the top line (on the bit), but also general obedience and response to the aids.

Synchrony

Refers to all riders turning at the same moment in individual movements, such as: left and right individual circles and half circles. Everyone must start and finish at the same time. Alignment is very often is dependant on synchrony and that is the reason why, in the Collective Marks on the test sheet that the two are scored together.

Thread the Needle

A movement in which riders coming single file from the corners of the arena, cross each others' path alternately on the center line.

The USDF has two quadrille tests at each level. Introductory Level, Tests 1 and 2 introduces new quadrille riders to riding simple movements as a group in the walk and trot. Novice Tests 1 and 2 include movements and transitions in walk, trot and canter. The Preliminary quadrille tests have a higher training requirement than the Novice tests, however, technically, the work is still equivalent to USAE First Level although this level is expected to show increased quality of impulsion, submission and performance as a team.

Currently the top quadrille level is called the Intermediate level. This is a more advanced level and the horses need to be secure in all the Second Level USAE tests. It also demands more complex formations at the walk, trot and canter. At the Intermediate level the teamwork is more demanding, with the team maintaining even spacing and performing movements in a correct and uniform manner.

Quadrilles for Fun

Quadrilles are fun and are well worth the effort if you wish to show at the current USDF quadrille levels. However, as with the regular musical freestyle you do not have to show and compete unless you wish. Do not be put off the idea of performing quadrilles just because you do not wish to compete. As long as you have a small group of like-minded folk at your barn you can start working together as a team. Look up the various movements and patterns in the index at the back of the book and start to enjoy riding together as a group. Ride in pairs, single file and all abreast. Try threading the needle (at the walk at first!). I have seen some interesting predicaments when inexperienced riders have tried this at the trot. But, making mistakes it is all part of the fun.

Once you have practiced some of the movements as a group, put together a simple quadrille of your own design or use one of the USDF tests. Practice the movements many times and perhaps organize a small exhibition at your barn or at a local show arena. Invite family, friends and supporters, show off, enjoy and have a party.

Overall the benefits are significant. And maybe you will find you want to compete anyway!

Pas de Deux

The pas de deux—two horse and rider combinations—is another interesting adventure for the dressage enthusiast. Practicing with a pair of horses that are agreeable can greatly benefit your basic riding skills much as in the same way as discussed for quadrilles. The big difference between training by yourself and training with another person in tandem is your ability to cope with the additional horse and rider. This can be harder than it seems. It is difficult enough to turn right and left and to ride a round circle by yourself. It is much more difficult to ride these movements with another horse, while keeping in pair formation and executing technically correct movements.

Riding in pairs with a friend will help you to relax and you might find the results amazing. Suddenly shoulders relax, wrists soften, fingers grip correctly and firmly, the head comes up by necessity just to see where you are going, the seat softens and the sitting trot suddenly becomes very easy to sit. Legs begin to hang down and relax, which makes the driving aids and the half halts easier to execute. Overall you could pay a fortune to a good trainer to assist in getting these results.

When you add music to the above equation the riding benefits will be doubled if not trebled. Swinging along to great trot tunes which match your horses' strides make riding so much easier and simpler. In some cases, the horses' timed gaits may not exactly match. If this is so, choose the timing that is the best compromise for both and regulate the individual horse's tempo to match. Once again, this has a great training benefit as the rider learns to regulate the gait.

This may be as far as you wish to go in your efforts to improve your riding by training in pairs to music. However, the USDF does offer pas de deux tests. These can be offered at any schooling or recognized show within the United States. If your local chapter does not offer the pas de deux, make your request known to the committee. They will probably make every effort to accommodate your wishes. Better still, whip up some enthusiasm and try to interest several riders in showing in this unique and interesting event.

The Pas de Deux in Competition

The pas de deux is a true freestyle where you choose the music, the patterns and movements that you which to perform. Just as in a regular freestyle, your pas de deux should have a theme and tell a story. Successful upper level pas de deux have included the strictly formal shad belly and top hat. If you choose, say, "West Side Story," you could add a rose on the shad belly and later the full bloom rose can be held in the teeth for good effect for some of the very Spanish moves.

Props are allowed to a degree. Because pas de deux competitions are still considered exhibitions, you can have colored polo wraps. Saddle pads of various colors or bearing velvet seams or emblems that help tell the story can be used. Bridles can have matching browbands or emblems at the throatlatch junction. Sparkles can be lightly sprinkled on rumps and hooves. I have seen a pas de deux ridden with both horses wearing breast plates (which are allowed) and at the center of the chest was a big bow and smiley face. A note here: costumes can only be worn in exhibitions or if the management allows costumes. In regular pas de deux competitions sanctioned by the USDF, the rider can add to the regulation tack and clothing required. Hence tartan shawls and polo wraps are OK as are, say, black "sunnies" or a black patch over the eyes that makes the wearer look like the robber in the particular pas de deux.

The old cat and mouse game was shown beautifully in a pas de deux to the music of nursery rhymes, including "Hickory Dickory Doc." A similar theme was a cop and robber pas de deux to music from the movie Rambo. A Scottish theme with tartan shawls on the riders and tartan bandages on the horses looked spectacular to music such as "Donald Where's Your Trousers" and "You Take the High Road."

USDF tests for the pas de deux are not broken down in to different levels as they are for quadrilles. Instead, you need to choose a comfortable level for both horses and riders. Select movements that the two of you can show easily and fluently. Some of the movements discussed in the section on quadrilles can be adapted and incorporated into your choreography such as thread the needle, cloverleaf, concentric circles and serpentines.

Working with just two horses you have greater flexibility to design both work in pairs and work in mirror images. In pairs, single file and in mirror image you can show various movements. Shoulder-in and travers down the centerline look great with the horses in pairs, with one showing shoulder-in right and the other shoulder-in left. Also effective is proceeding on the centerline line in single file and show the shoulder-in, one horse to the left and the other to the right. You can also show these movements on the long sides or quarter lines in pairs, single file and in mirror image. Experiment and design various patterns and try them out and see if they work, making sure they blend with your choice of music. Production and design of the pas de deux can be fun and a good learning experience.

The pas de deux event itself is similar to the musical freestyle tests. The judging is based on two sections: Technical and Artistic Impression. Each section has the same total marks.

The **technical** work is broken down to three major sections:

1. **Performance** as a pair is very important. Remember you are a team and try to show your control and training by working together in harmony.

2. **Accuracy** of the movements in the technical section also reflects the marks given for the pair performance. If one horse lacks bend or is not straight on straight lines, this must be noted as it disturbs the accuracy of the performance.

3. **The submission** of the two horses is judged in with the impulsion evaluation. The horses must perform the freestyle pas de deux in a forward and fluent fashion so that the audience and judge are all tapping along with the music. If one of the horses shows a resistance such as head tossing or spooking, it detracts from the overall performance.

On the **artistic** side, there are also three sections:

1. **Choreography,** which includes balanced and geometric patterns, should show creativity in design and if possible a degree of difficulty in the execution. Keep the choreography bright, forward, interesting and inventive but within your horses' capabilities.

2. ***Harmony*** between horses and riders. This section is also linked to the technical side, particularly to the technical aspects of submission and accuracy.

3. ***Musicality.*** Does the music suit the horses and their gaits? Does the music address the theme of the pas de deux? If your chosen trot music is "The Yellow Rose of Texas," you may choose to have tiny yellow ribbons in the braids or brow bands and/or saddle pads. Themes from the old movies of *Camelot* and *Showboat* can show lots of creative individuality. Choose a theme and music of your choice and develop it into an individual expression of your own creative abilities.
Most of all have fun and enjoy the experience.

Exhibition Rides

Exhibition rides are not well documented in current literature, but ever since man has taken to the backs of horses, there have been some sort of riding exhibitions.

Exhibition rides continued to promote various equestrian sports that were not included in quadrilles and pas des deux. In the nineteenth and twentieth centuries, exhibition rides have showed the beauty of the various equestrian sports and disciplines by highlighting their breed, the costumes, the skills of their equestrian disciple and the associated traditions of their chosen sport. These displays have included the versatility of the Quarter Horse, with his agile spin and slides to Indian ponies showing their traditional themes in costume, music and great riding skills, to the grace of sidesaddle exhibitions and spirited Arabian horses showing off the their desert ancestry.

Exhibitions can also highlight the horse and rider dancing

The Lion King himself! It's actually Rebecca Langwost and Gomerant, performing at the 2002 USDF Freestyle Symposium.

Photo by Reg Corkum

a theme from either musicals or movies. An example of this is the use of the story from the popular Disney movie, *The Lion King* at the USDF Musical Freestyle Symposium in 2002. This was a spectacular theatrical performance involving over 20 different riders that left spectators cheering and on their feet at the end. This was equestrian theatre at its best . . .breathtaking and moving!

Chapter 11

Kids and Freestyles

Leigh Ann Hazel-Groux

*B*agels and lox. Peanut butter and jelly. Green eggs and ham. Kids and ponies. What could be better combination? Kids, ponies and freestyles. Truly!

One cannot argue that most children have a natural affinity for music. Who has not seen even a very young child dance uninhibitedly to any sort of rhythm? Add a pony to this enthusiasm and the result can be very special and joyful indeed.

While there have been those who say that freestyles should not be attempted until a rider has achieved at least Third Level, there is merit, I believe, for a rider to learn the basics of riding and how it relates to music sooner rather than later. This rider has a head start on understanding and enjoying freestyles.

The United States Pony Clubs (USPC), established in 1954, is one of America's chief organizations that teaches and equips junior riders with the skills and knowledge necessary for a lifetime enjoyment of horses. Initially, the original Pony Club competition was centered around the three-day event, with riders participating in all three phases: dressage, cross country and stadium jumping. In the mid-1980s, the competitions were expanded at the regional and national levels to include not only eventing, but also individual competitions focused solely on dressage or stadium jumping.

Beginning in the early 1990s, USPC incorporated freestyles into the dressage portion of rallies at both the regional and national levels. These freestyle events, which

Kids and ponies just go together.
Here is Brian Whitford and Blue Girl.

included both individual rides and pas des deux, were performed at Training, First and Second Levels, broken down by test numbers (i.e., 1, 2, 3 and 4) within each level. Most regional rallies require that children wishing to qualify for the National Championships must perform a freestyle.

At the 2001 National Pony Club Championships, dressage was the largest division. Within it, there were 140 freestyle rides. The top two honors went to a Training Level ride and a Fourth Level ride. As of 2002, the dressage division offers a new breakout of divisions: Training Level, First Level and Second Level and above. Quadrille is also offered to any Pony Clubbers who can put together a team.

USAE "S" judge Trip Harting, himself a former "A" Pony Clubber, is an ardent supporter of freestyles. It was through Harting's urging that freestyle became a part of the Pony Club competitions. He believes that encouraging children to learn to ride with music—and more specifically to do this within the context of quadrille and pas de deux—reinforces the importance of developing the basic skills of riding and controlling the horse, while enjoying the camaraderie and fun of working as a team.

In an article titled, "How Could Dressage Be Boring?" published in *Dressage Today*, Harting points out that just as children start out learning social skills in school, they learn as a group by performing quadrilles. As they master the skills necessary to succeed, they become more inspired and move on to performing pas des deux and eventually to solo rides.

Harting's ultimate goal is to produce a generation of junior riders who, at an early age, begin developing experience with freestyles. This experience would equip them to be further ahead on the learning curve as they grow older and enter both the Young Rider programs, where they must now perform a freestyle at the Prix. St. Georges level, and later the adult ranks as seasoned freestyle riders. Riding freestyles also will help to encourage their enthusiasm for dressage and keep the sport growing.

This enthusiasm is quite a force among those Pony Clubbers who become involved with freestyles. They bring a freshness and openness along with innovation and creative thinking to the process that makes it quite fun to work with them. Sometimes, it may be the style of music they have chosen, while at other times, they can offer new twists on the required movements.

One group of Pony Clubbers I worked with was quite enterprising. I would conduct one-day clinics for them. During the clinic, we would establish the beats per minute of their horse and by working with a large selection of sample music, determine the style that best suited each of them. When each session was done, I would give each child the name of the album(s) and/or artist that was selected for them and some advice on the best way to go about creating their tape and choreography. Using this information, the kids created their own freestyles and took them to Rally. I heard back from many of them who subsequently had fun and successful rides. Kudos to those kids and their parents for such effort and dedication!

One of my fondest memories is of a junior rider who was a D-1 level Pony Clubber (about 6 years old) who came to me during a "fix-a-test" clinic prior to attending her Rally. Her pony looked like it had come straight off the pages of *Thelwell's Riding Academy* and while her tack might not have been the newest, it was clean and well turned out. The music she had chosen was "I Just Can't Wait to Be King" from the Disney movie *The Lion King*. Her level was Pre-Training, meaning the ride consisted of walk, trot and 20 meter circles. She had choreographed the ride herself. When the music started, she came trotting confidently into the ring; the joy in what she was doing was evident. As the ride progressed, she began singing the song to herself and actually closed her eyes. I dare anyone who was present to say it was boring or not well done or entertaining!

While singing and closing one's eyes is not the generally recommended way to perform freestyles, my main point is this: Even though Pony Clubbers may be performing freestyles at the lowest levels, they can still be well-ridden, creatively choreographed and enjoyable to watch. What each child is learning can be used throughout their riding career, namely the correct basics of riding, how to learn and keep a regular rhythm, the creativeness of choreography and the confidence in presentation.

Even if a child isn't going to ride a freestyle, working with music is a wonderful way to teach regularity of rhythm. As Harting said about quadrilles, riding to a specific tempo in a group setting can often teach more about controlling a pony's gaits that 10 hours of verbal lessons could accomplish.

If a child often rides alone in a ring, a parent can help by making a practice tape that can be played during this time. This way, the child can learn to listen to music and hear the beat as well as experiment with choreography, putting together movements while he or she schools. While no "formal" freestyle may be in the immediate future, this is a good way to prepare for the day when one may be required.

Chapter 12

The Future of the Musical Freestyle

Libby Anderson

The twenty-first century has dawned, and the new millennium has proven challenging, unexpected and unpredictable. From the terrorist attacks on Sept. 11, 2001, to the dreaded Foot and Mouth Disease in the United Kingdom, the world seems divided by race, religion, war and disease. One unexpected event after another seems to tumble upon us. Yet, despite the turmoil and economic downturn, interest in equestrian sports has held steady and has even increased as more people turn to the noble horse as a means of sport and recreation.

Currently, dressage participation is on the rise in the United States. This is due to several factors: the wonderful dressage programs offered by the USDF, the Young Rider scholarships given by the USDF, USAE and various foundations, the success of the USA dressage riders in overseas international competitions, including the Olympic Games, World Equestrian Games and the Freestyle World Cup have also helped to boost enthusiasm. Overall, the grass roots efforts of the USDF, and many local dressage regions and chapters all over the United States, have culminated in a thriving dressage community.

As we have seen, classical dressage is an age-old discipline that, despite world changes, has changed very little in itself. The delight of watching and participating in a sport that highlights the harmony, trust, balance, strength and beauty of the horse extends from the basics of training through the preciseness of the Grand Prix. Those who are dressage devotees hardly need additional incentive. However, we enter a century that functions largely through the instant media of televisions, satellites, cell phones, video and the Internet. In light of that, in order to spark continued interest in such a classical sport, the FEI and the national federations recognize the need to bring dressage to the masses in such a way as can be enjoyed and appreciated—enter the freestyle.

During the past decade, musical freestyle has blended the beauty and sensitivity of classical dressage with the excitement and magic of music. The success with which this has been done has certainly highlighted freestyle to be the future of dressage. This was definitely the case as shown by the debut of the freestyle in competition at the Atlanta Olympics in 1996. Suddenly the must-have ticket was to the final freestyle competition, with attendance matching or outselling the always popular show jumping. Crowds cheered, the cameras and TV personnel were hard at work and the sponsor booths and horse emporiums had a very busy trade. What a success for modern dressage!

The resulting enthusiasm has spawned more competitions, dressage clinics, workshops, symposia and forums. A surge of excitement has taken over in the musical freestyle arena, and the freestyle has blossomed together with a real appreciation of the musical score, choreography and artistic merit. Freestyle forums are offered for riders, trainers, judges, choreographers and musicians, supported by continuing education and clinics for the horse and rider.

To conclude this book on the musical freestyle, we need to reflect on the great changes that have been made in the freestyle in the past few years. At one time, the USDF musical freestyles used to be more or less a consolation class for riders who were not really up to correctly riding the regular tests. Now, in only a few short years, we perhaps forget much of the history and rule-making that has occurred in the evolution of musical freestyle. Today it maintains a consistent quality and is certainly easier to judge as a result. Overall, it is generally agreed that these changes have improved the quality and quantity of USDF musical freestyle rides.

The degree of difficulty in both the FEI freestyle tests is now also well defined and clarified. Linda Zang, FEI "O" Dressage Judge and USA freestyle guru has mentioned that as of 2003 the scores from all FEI tests will be given in percentages only. The role of the FEI Freestyle Committee is to continue to evaluate all the complicated and intricate movements allowed in the musical freestyle, to keep classical dressage alive and well and to prevent any aspect of circus from entering the freestyle arena.

The freestyle has come of age, both in the United States and in Europe. There is a place, now, for everyone in our sport, and we are secure in the knowledge that we can enjoy every aspect that dressage has to offer and maybe specialize in one particular niche. It may be quadrille, exhibitions or straight dressage tests. Whatever is your love and your passion, in this sport we can offer you good competition, good training and a guarantee that the musical freestyle will grow and thrive in the years to come.

Viva la freestyle!

Appendix I

Official Score Sheets

Musical Freestyle First Level

TECHNICAL EXECUTION

NOTE: *Movements which must be performed on both hands are so indicated by a dotted line under "Preliminary Notes." Omitted compulsory movements receive a "0" and are averaged into the "Judges Marks." Judges marks for Technical Execution must be given in half points or full points (no tenths).

TIME MAXIMUM: **5 minutes**

COMPULSORY MOVEMENTS	POSSIBLE POINTS	PRELIMINARY NOTES		JUDGE'S MARK	CO-EFFICIENT	FINAL SCORE	REMARKS
1. Walk (20M minimum continuous Freewalk)	10				2		
2. 10-meter circle in trot*	10	L	R				
3. Leg-yield in trot*	10	L	R		2		
4. Lengthen stride in trot	10				2		
5. 15-meter circle in canter*	10	L	R				
6. Change of lead through trot*	10	L	R		2		
7. Lengthen stride in canter	10				2		

Further Remarks:

SUBTOTAL

DEDUCTIONS

TOTAL TECHNICAL EXECUTION
(120 total possible)

FIRST LEVEL

Clearly Forbidden
• Reinback
• Shoulder-in
• Travers
• Renvers
• Half-pass
• Flying changes
• Turn on haunches or Pirouette (walk or canter)
• Piaffe
• Passage

Clearly Allowed
• Counter canter
• Zig-zag leg yield
• Leg yield along wall
• Lengthen trot or canter on 20m circle
• Canter serpentine
• Simple change
• Change of lead through trot
• Walk-canter-walk-canter
• Halt-canter-halt-canter

Forbidden and Allowed: Movements "above the level" (found ONLY in a higher level test) receive a deduction of four points from Total Technical Execution for each illegal movement, but not for each recurrence of the same movement. All figures (regardless of size), patterns, combination or transitions composed of elements permitted in the declared level ARE permitted, even if the resulting configuration is found in higher levels. To serve as guidelines, the adjacent lists specifically enumerate most of the dressage movements, combinations and transitions which are forbidden or allowed at each level.

ARTISTIC IMPRESSION

NOTE: Non-compulsory movements must be rewarded or penalized under "Choreography" and/or "Degree of Difficulty" (Artistic). Movements "Above the Level" are not rewarded in Artistic Impression. Judges marks for Artistic Impression must be given in half points or full points (no tenths).

NO.

	POSSIBLE POINTS	JUDGE'S MARKS	CO-EFFICIENT	FINAL MARKS	REMARKS
1. Rhythm, energy and elasticity	10		2		
2. Harmony between horse and rider	10		2		
3. Choreography, use of arena, inventiveness, design cohesiveness, balance, ingenuity and creativity	10		3		
4. Degree of difficulty	10		1		
5. Choice of music & interpretation of music	10		4		

Further Remarks:

SUBTOTAL	
DEDUCTIONS	
TOTAL ARTISTIC IMPRESSION (120 total possible)	
TOTAL TECHNICAL EXECUTION (120 total possible)	
FINAL SCORE (240 total possible)	
PERCENTAGE (Final Score divided by 240)	

Deductions:
▼ Exceeding the time limit = 2 points from Total Artistic Impression.
▼ Movements "Above the Level" = 4 points from Total Technical Execution for each illegal movement, but not for each recurrence of the same movement.

In Case of a Tie: The higher total for Artistic Impression will break the tie.

Reprinted by the kind permission of the USDF.
© 2001 United States Dressage Federation

Musical Freestyle Second Level

Editor's Note: *The Artistic Impression score sheet is the same for First, Second, Third and Fourth levels*

TECHNICAL EXECUTION

NOTE: *Movements which must be performed on both hands are so indicated by a dotted line under "Preliminary Notes." Omitted compulsory movements receive a "O" and are averaged into the "Judges Marks." Judges marks for Technical Execution must be given in half points or full points (no tenths).

TIME MAXIMUM: **5 minutes**

SECOND LEVEL

COMPULSORY MOVEMENTS	POSSIBLE POINTS	PRELIMINARY NOTES		JUDGE'S MARK	CO-EFFICIENT	FINAL SCORE	REMARKS
1. Walk (20M minimum continuous Freewalk)	10				2		
2. Shoulder-in at trot*	10	L	R		2		
3. *Travers and/or Renvers at trot*	10	L	R		2		
4. Medium trot	10				2		
5. 10-meter circle in canter*	10	L	R				
6. Simple change of lead*	10	L	R		2		
7. Medium canter	10						

*At least one must be shown in both directions.

Further Remarks:

SUBTOTAL	
DEDUCTIONS	
TOTAL TECHNICAL EXECUTION (120 total possible)	

Musical Freestyle Third Level

TECHNICAL EXECUTION

NOTE: *Movements which must be performed on both hands are so indicated by a dotted line under "Preliminary Notes." Omitted compulsory movements receive a "O" and are averaged into the "Judges Marks." Judges marks for Technical Execution must be given in half points or full points (no tenths).

TIME MAXIMUM:
5 minutes

THIRD LEVEL

COMPULSORY MOVEMENTS	POSSIBLE POINTS	PRELIMINARY NOTES		JUDGE'S MARK	CO-EFFICIENT	FINAL SCORE	REMARKS
1. Walk (20M minimum continuous Extended)	10				2		
2. Shoulder-in*	10	L	R				
3. Trot Half-pass*	10	L	R		2		
4. Extended trot	10						
5. Canter Half-pass*	10	L	R		2		
6. Counter canter*	10	L	R				
7. Flying change of lead*	10	L	R		2		
8. Extended canter	10						

Further Remarks:

SUBTOTAL

DEDUCTIONS

TOTAL TECHNICAL EXECUTION
(120 total possible)

THIRD LEVEL

Clearly Forbidden
- Tempi changes (4s, 3s, 2s, 1s)
- Canter Pirouette
- Piaffe
- Passage

Clearly Allowed
- Everything that is not clearly forbidden, including:
- Half-pass zig-zag in trot
- Half-pass zig-zag in canter with flying changes
- Full and double walk pirouette

Forbidden and Allowed: Movements "above the level" (found ONLY in a higher level test) receive a deduction of four points from Total Technical Execution for each illegal movement, but not for each recurrence of the same movement. All figures (regardless of size), patterns, combination or transitions composed of elements permitted in the declared level ARE permitted, even if the resulting configuration is found in higher levels. To serve as guidelines, the adjacent lists specifically enumerate most of the dressage movements, combinations and transitions which are forbidden or allowed at each level.

Reprinted by the kind permission of the USDF.
© 2001 United States Dressage Federation

Musical Freestyle Fourth Level

Editor's Note: *The Artistic Impression score sheet is the same for First, Second, Third and Fourth levels*

TECHNICAL EXECUTION

NOTE: *Movements which must be performed on both hands are so indicated by a dotted line under "Preliminary Notes." Omitted compulsory movements receive a "O" and are averaged into the "Judges Marks." Judges marks for Technical Execution must be given in half points or full points (no tenths).

TIME MAXIMUM: 5 minutes

FOURTH LEVEL

COMPULSORY MOVEMENTS	POSSIBLE POINTS	PRELIMINARY NOTES		JUDGE'S MARK	CO-EFFICIENT	FINAL SCORE	REMARKS
1. Walk (20M minimum continuous Collected)	10						
2. Walk (20M minimum continuous Extended)	10						
3. Trot Half-pass*	10	L	R		2		
4. Extended trot	10						
5. Shoulder-in*	10	L	R				
6. Canter Half-pass*	10	L	R				
7. Extended canter	10						
8. Flying changes of lead, every third stride (3 min.)	10				2		
9. Canter Half-pirouette*	10	L	R		2		

Further Remarks:

SUBTOTAL	
DEDUCTIONS	
TOTAL TECHNICAL EXECUTION (120 total possible)	

FOURTH LEVEL

Clearly Forbidden
• Full Canter Pirouette
• Tempi changes (2s, 1s)
• Piaffe
• Passage

Clearly Allowed
• Everything that is not clearly forbidden

Forbidden and Allowed: Movements "above the level" (found ONLY in a higher level test) receive a deduction of four points from Total Technical Execution for each illegal movement, but not for each recurrence of the same movement. All figures (regardless of size), patterns, combination or transitions composed of elements permitted in the declared level ARE permitted, even if the resulting configuration is found in higher levels. To serve as guidelines, the adjacent lists specifically enumerate most of the dressage movements, combinations and transitions which are forbidden or allowed at each level.

Reprinted by the kind permission of the USDF.
© 2001 United States Dressage Federation

FEI Intermediate 1
Freestyle Test 2002

Time allowed: performance to be finished between 4'30" and 5'00"

Technical	1	Collected walk (minimum 20m)
	2	Extended walk (minimum 20m)
	3	Collected trot including shoulder-in right
	4	Collected trot including shoulder-in left
	5	Collected trot including half-pass right
	6	Collected trot including half-pass left
	7	Extended trot
	8	Collected canter
	9	Collected canter including half-pass right
	10	Collected canter including half-pass left
	11	Extended canter
	12	Flying changes every third stride (minimum 5 times consecutively)
	13	Flying changes every second stride (minimum 5 times consecutively)
	14	Single pirouette in canter right
	15	Single pirouette in canter left
Artistic	16	Rhythm, energy and elasticity
	17	Harmony between rider and horse
	18	Choreography, Use of arena. Inventiveness
	19	Degree of difficulty. Calculated risks
	20	Music and interpretation of the music
	Total points =	**400**

Movements of a higher level are not allowed. However, travers, renvers and half pirouettes are allowed.
Time penalty: more than 5' or less than 4'30" deduct 2 points from the total of artistic presentation.
In case two competitors have the same final score, the one with the higher marks for artistic impression will have the better placing.

Edition 1988/Revision 2002
Copyright©2002
Fédération Equestre Internationale
Reproduction strictly reserved

Reprinted by the kind permission of the FEI.
© 2002 Fédération Equestre Internationale

1999 Grand Prix Freestyle

	Technical Marks	Marks	Points	Coefficient	Final Marks	Remarks
1.	Collected walk (minimum 20 m).	10				
2.	Extended walk (minimum 20 m).	10				
3.	Collected trot including half-pass right.	10				
4.	Collected trot including half-pass left.	10				
5.	Extended trot.	10				
6.	Collected canter including half-pass right.	10				
7.	Collected canter including half-pass left.	10				
8.	Extended canter.	10				
9.	Flying changes every second stride (minimum 5 times consecutively)	10				
10.	Flying changes every stride (minimum 9 times consecutively)	10				
11.	Canter pirouette right.	10		2		
12.	Canter pirouette left.	10		2		
13.	Passage (minimum 20m).	10		2		
14.	Piaffe (minimum 10 steps).	10		2		
15.	Transitions from passage to piaffe and from piaffe to passage.					
	Total for Technical Executions	200				
	Artistic Marks*					
16.	Rhythm, energy and elasticity.	10		3		
17.	Harmony between rider and horse.	10		3		
18.	Choreography. Use of arena. Inventiveness.	10		4		
19.	Degree of difficulty. Well calculated risks.	10		4		
20.	Choice of music and interpretation of the music.	10		6		
	Total for Artistic Presentation	200				

*half points may be given

To Be Deducted
Time penalty: more than 6 minutes or less than 5 minutes 30 seconds, deduct 2 points form the total artistic presentation.

Score (see conversion table)

Total for technical execution divided by 20	10		
Total for artistic presentation divided by 20	10		
Final Score	20		

World Cup
   In case two competitors have the same final score, the one with the higher marks for artistic impression is leading.
CDI***
   In case two competitors have the same final score, the one with the higher technical mark is leading.

Reprinted by the kind permission of the FEI.
© 1995 Fédération Equestre Internationale

FEI Young Riders
Freestyle Test 2002

Time allowed: performance to be finished between 4'30" and 5'00"

Technical	1	Collected walk (minimum 20m)
	2	Extended walk (minimum 20m)
	3	Collected trot including shoulder-in right
	4	Collected trot including shoulder-in left
	5	Collected trot including half-pass right
	6	Collected trot including half-pass left
	7	Extended trot
	8	Collected canter
	9	Collected canter including half-pass right
	10	Collected canter including half-pass left
	11	Extended canter
	12	Flying changes every fourth stride (minimum 5 times consecutively)
	13	Flying changes every third stride (minimum 5 times consecutively)
	14	Half pirouette in canter right
	15	Half pirouette in canter left
	Total for technical execution =	**200**

Movements of a higher level are not allowed, travers and renvers are allowed.

Artistic	16	Rhythm, energy and elasticity
	17	Harmony between rider and horse
	18	Choreography, Use of arena. Inventiveness
	19	Degree of difficulty. Calculated risks
	20	Music and interpretation of the music
	Total for artistic presentation =	**200**

To be deducted

Time penalty: more than 5' or less than 4'30" deduct 2 points from the total of artistic presentation.
In case two competitors have the same final score, the one with the higher marks for artistic impression will have the better placing.

Edition 1988/Revision 2002
Copyright©2002
Fédération Equestre Internationale
Reproduction strictly reserved

1996 PAS de DEUX

Competiton

No.

Date   Judge

No.

Team Name

	SCORE (1-10)	COEFFICiENT	TOTAL
TECHNICAL EXECUTION			
1. Performance as a pair			
2. Accurary of Execution			
3. Implusion & Submission			
ARTISTIC IMPRESSION			
1. Choreography *balance, creativity, difficulty, construction*			
2. Harmony Between Horses & Riders, Fluency of Performance			
3. Musicality			

Time Allowed: 5 minutes

All Levels

Total points: 200

   Half-points (.5) are allowed

Comments:

SCORE _____

DEDUCTIONS _____

FINAL SCORE _____

PERCENTAGE _____

Published by:
United States Dressage Federation
P.O. Box 6669
Lincoln, NE 68506-0669
January 1996

Judges' Signature _____

Reprinted by the kind permission of the USDF.
© 1996 United States Dressage Federation

Quadrille Tests

1996

USDF PRELIMINARY QUADRILLE TEST 1
1 9 9 6
NO.

Name of Competition _____
Team _____
PURPOSE To perform with inc

1999 USDF PRELIMINARY QUADRILLE TEST 2 | NO.

Name of Competition _____ Date _____
Team _____ Judge _____
PURPOSE: 1. To test a quadrille's ability to perform more difficult patterns at the preliminary level, to perform pairs work at the trot, to demonstrate more lateral work (leg-yielding) and lengthening of the stride at the trot. 2. Emphasis on continued importance of performing movements with accurate syncrony

---

1996

USDF NOVICE QUADRILLE TEST 1
1 9 9 6
NO.

Name of Competition _____
Team _____
PURPOSE: To exhibit movements
riders' aids.
CONDITIONS: Arena 20 m x 4

1996

USDF NOVICE QUADRILLE TEST 2
1 9 9 6
NO.

Name of Competition _____ Date _____
Team _____ Judge _____
PURPOSE: To exhibit movements and transitions at walk, trot and canter. Horses should move energetically forward at a even tempo and accept the
riders' aids

1996

USDF INTRODUCTORY QUADRILLE TEST 2
1 9 9 6
NO.

Name of Competition _____
Team _____
PURPOSE: To introduce the qu
manner.
CONDITIONS: Arena 20 m x 4

1996

USDF INTRODUCTORY QUADRILLE TEST 1
1 9 9 6
NO.

Name of Competition _____ Date _____
Team _____ Judge _____
PURPOSE: To introduce the quadrille team to competition. Test is be performed at a walk and trot only, in a calm, obedient, uniform manner.

1996

USDF INTERMEDIATE QUADRILLE TEST 1
1 9 9 6
NO.

Name of Competition _____
Team _____
PURPOSE: To exhibit Second
calm, obedient, moving freely a
movements in a uniform manne
CONDITIONS: Arena 20 m x 4

1999 USDF INTERMEDIATE QUADRILLE TEST 2 | NO.

Name of Competition _____ Date _____
Team _____ Judge _____
PURPOSE: To test a quadrille's ability to perform more difficult patterns at the intermediate level, to perform pairs work at the canter, to demonstrate shoulder-in, counter canter, and canter simple changes, and turns on the haunches. Emphasis on continued importance of performing movements with accurate synchrony and alignment, and spacing.
CONDITIONS: Arena 20 m × 40 m • Unless otherwise noted, all trot work is to be ridden sitting.

Preliminary Quadrille Test 1

1996

USDF PRELIMINARY QUADRILLE TEST 1	1996	NO.

Name of Competition _____ Date _____

Team _____ Judge _____

PURPOSE: To perform with increased quality of impulsion, submission and performance as a team.

CONDITIONS: Arena 20 m x 40 m

> Wherever 1s & 2s are mentioned, it is in order to make an alternating separation clear. Each team may decide which order it prefers.

		TEST	POINTS	COEFFICIENT	TOTAL	REMARKS
1.	A X C	Enter at working trot in pairs Halt in fan formation; salute Proceed at working trot in pairs Divide				
2.	H & M	Oblique to centerline to form pairs				
3.	When on Center Line A	Individual 10 m circles (1's left, 2's right) Divide				
4.	FXH & KXM C	Change rein and thread the needle, 1's in front of 2's Cross over				
5.	B & E E & B	When centered on long sides, individual left and right turns; pass through on centerline Individual right and left turns onto long sides — all heading toward A				
6.	A D-M & D-H C	Down centerline single file, 1's before 2's Leg yield, alternately right & left Cross over				
7.	E & B Before C	Columns half circle to centerline to form pairs Walk				
8.	C E	Column of pairs turn left Column half circle left onto centerline Column half circle right onto long side				
9.	F K E M	Trot (as one) Outside file K-E; inside file K-B Outside file E-M; inside file B-M Form single line				
10.	C	Canter, left lead and circle 20m				
11.	HXF	Change rein, at X trot individually				
12.	A	Canter, right lead, and circle t 20 m				
13.	KXM	Change rein, at X trot individually				
14.	Betw H & K Betw M & F	Left turn, individually Right turn, individually				
15.	F	Form pairs in corner				
16.	A	Down centerline Halt in fan formation; salute Leave arena at walk				

Reprinted by the kind permission of the USDF.
© 2001 United States Dressage Federation

COLLECTIVE MARKS:

17.	Spacing					
18.	Synchrony & Alignment					
19.	Impulsion					
20.	Submission					
21	Performance As a Group		x2			

Total points possible: **220**

FURTHER REMARKS:

TOTAL POINTS _____

PERCENTAGE _____

Judge Signature _____

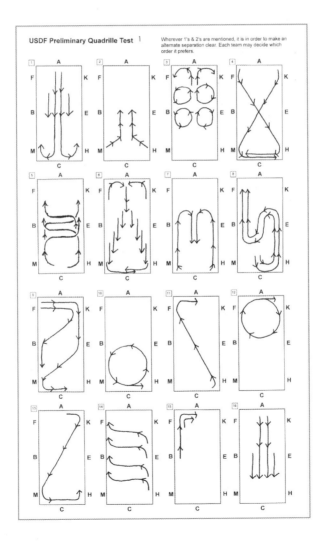

Intermediate Quadrille Test 2

1999 USDF INTERMEDIATE QUADRILLE TEST 2	NO.

Name of Competition_____ Date _____

Team_____ Judge _____

PURPOSE: To test a quadrille's ability to perform more difficult patterns at the intermediate level, to perform pairs work at the canter, to demonstrate shoulder-in, counter canter, and canter simple changes, and turns on the haunches. Emphasis on continued importance of performing movements with accurate synchrony and alignment, and spacing.

CONDITIONS: Arena 20 m × 40 m • Unless otherwise noted, all trot work is to be ridden sitting.

Whenever 1's & 2's are mentioned, it is in order to make an alternating separation clear. Each team may decide which order it prefers.

TEST		POINTS	COEFFICIENT	TOTAL	REMARKS
1. A X C	Enter collected trot in pairs. Halt, fan formation. Salute. Proceed collected trot in pairs. Divide.				
2. HXF & MXK F & K	Thread the needle, medium trot. Collected trot.				
3. Between F & A K & A	Columns right and left 10 M circles.				
4. A D to X Beyond X	Turn on centerline in pairs. Rt. and left shoulder-in in pairs. Individual right and left obliques to the rail.				
5. C Centered on E & B	Cross over. Individual right and left turns across the arena, passing through on the C/L. 1 & 2 track toward C 3 & 4 track toward A				
6. A & C Centered on X	Turn onto centerline forming pairs. Individual right and left 10 M circles, forming cloverleaf.				
7. X E & B A	Turn toward B & E. Turn toward A, forming single files. Turn onto centerline forming single file.				
8. Between D & X Centered on X	Walk altogether. Individual left obliques.				
9. Between E & H	Individual turns on the haunches, right, returning to the oblique line. Individual obliques to centerline.				
10. A Between A & F & A & K Centered on E & B	1's track right, 2's track left. Canter altogether. Individual right and left 10 M circles.				
11. C Between B & F E & K	Cross over. Individual 1/2 circles onto centerline, forming pairs (on opposite leads).				
12. C H—1/4 Marker before F M—1/4 Marker before K	Divide Thread the needle.				
13. Touching A B & E	1/2 20 M circles, holding the counter canter. Simple change of lead.				
14. C X	Turn onto centerline forming pairs. Files circle left and right 10 meters.				
15. A	Divide. Form pairs on corners.				
16. B to E & E to B	20 meter 1/2 circles in pairs.				
17. Betw. E & K B & F A G	Pairs trot. Turn onto centerline in pairs. Halt, fan formation. Salute.				

Reprinted by the kind permission of the USDF.
© 2001 United States Dressage Federation

18.	Spacing				
19.	Synchrony & Alignment				
20.	Impulsion				
21.	Submission				
22.	Performance As a Group		x2		

FURTHER REMARKS:

Judge Signature _____

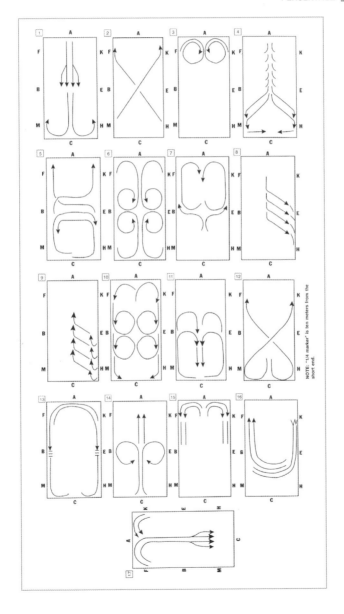

Appendix II

Official Organizations

1. *Fédération Equestre Internationale*
Avenue Mon Repos 24
P.O. Box 157
1000 Lausanne 5
Switzerland
Tel.: 41 21 310 47 47
info@horsesport.org

2. *USA Equestrian*
4047 Iron Works Parkway
Lexington, KY 40511-8483
(859) 258-2472
www.equestrian.org

3. *United States Dressage Federation*
220 Lexington Circle
Suite 510
Lexington, KY 50403
(859) 971-2277
www.usdf.org

4. *United States Pony Clubs, Inc.*
The Kentucky Horse Park
4071 Iron Works Pike
Lexington, KY 40511-8462
(606) 254-7669 (PONY)
uspc@mis.net

Appendix III

Choreography Patterns

1996 First Level Test 4 – Pony Club

Emily Weber and Kelly

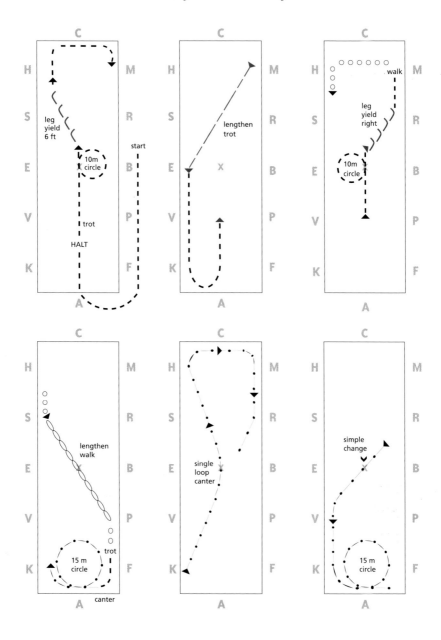

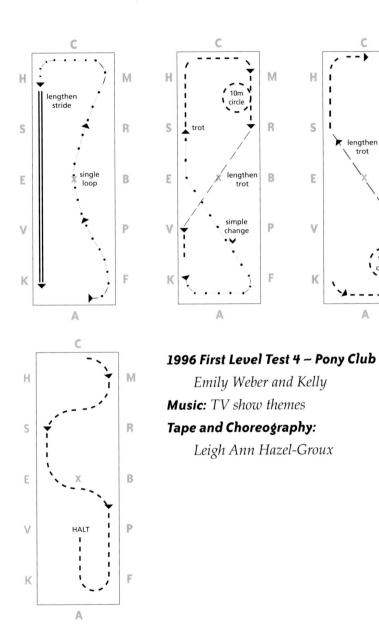

1996 First Level Test 4 – Pony Club

Emily Weber and Kelly

Music: *TV show themes*

Tape and Choreography:

Leigh Ann Hazel-Groux

2000 USDF First Level

Betsy Parker and Lane

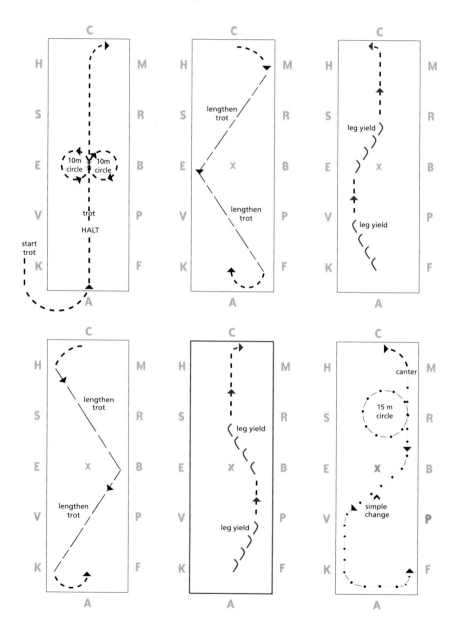

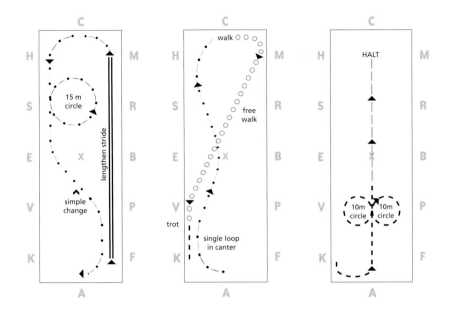

2000 USDF First Level

Betsy Parker and Lane

Music: *Latin (Herb Alpert)*

Tape and Choreography: *Leigh Ann Hazel-Groux*

2001 USDF Second Level

Jessie Ginsburg and Rhinecliff

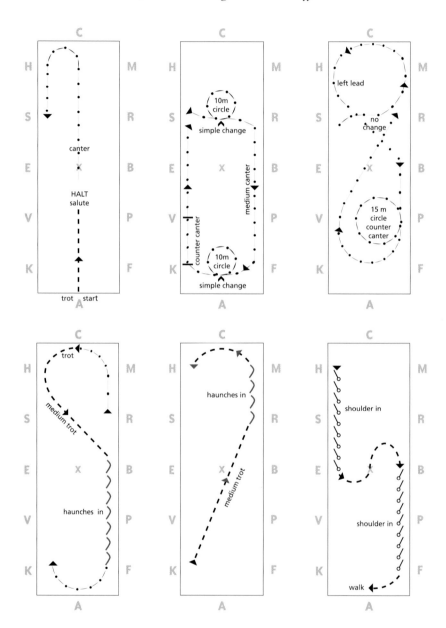

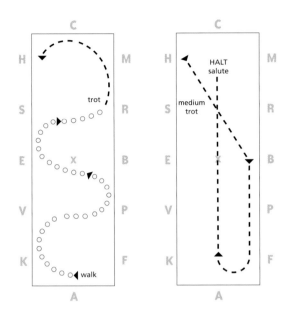

2001 USDF Second Level

Jessie Ginsburg and Rhinecliff

Music: *American Movie Westerns*

Tape and Choreography: *Leigh Ann Hazel-Groux*

2001 USDF Third Level

Tracey Lert and Luminary

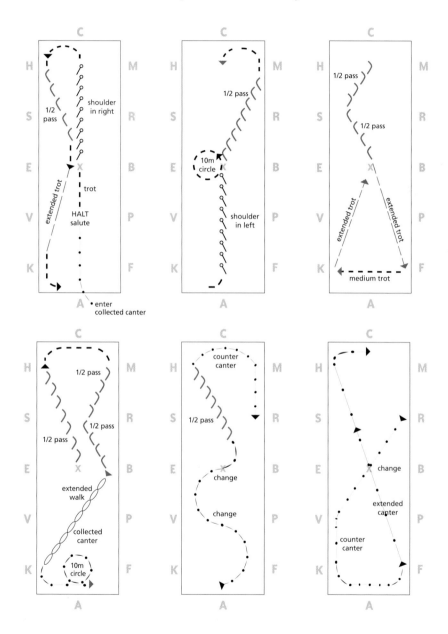

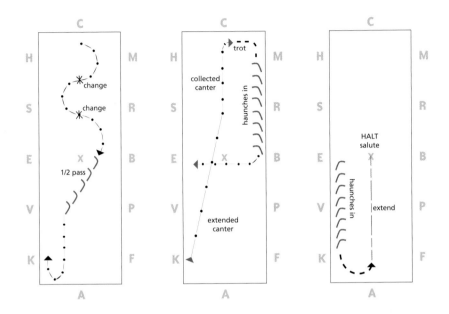

2001 USDF Third Level

Tracey Lert and Luminary

Music by: *Terry Ciotto-Gallo*

Tape and Choreography: *Tracey Lert*

2001 USDF Fourth Level

Tracey Lert and Lexus

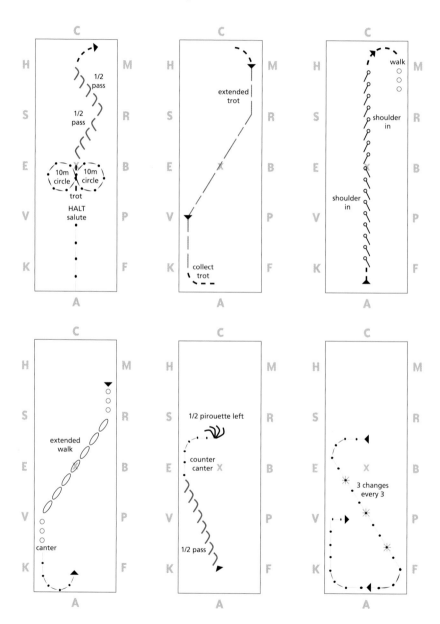

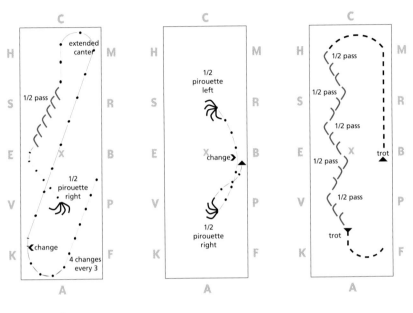

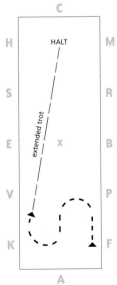

2001 USDF Fourth Level

Tracey Lert and Lexus

Music by:

Tape and Choreography:

187

1992 F.E.I. Intermediare I - Freestyle

Leigh Ann Hazel and Midas Touch

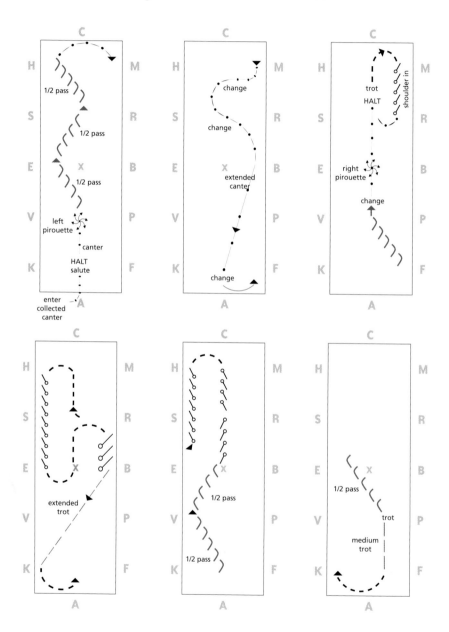

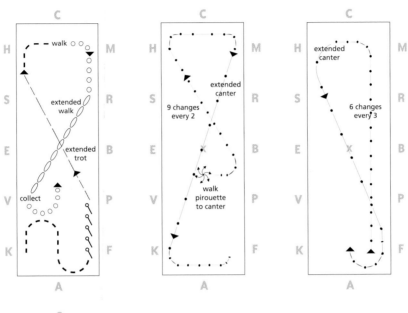

1992 F.E.I. Intermediare I - Freestyle

Leigh Ann Hazel and Midas Touch

Music: *Big Band (Irving Berlin)*

Tape by: *Mary Campbell*

Choreography: *Linda Oliver*

Grand Prix - 2000 Palm Beach Dressage Derby - Freestyle

Barbara Silverman and Chantor de Bounce

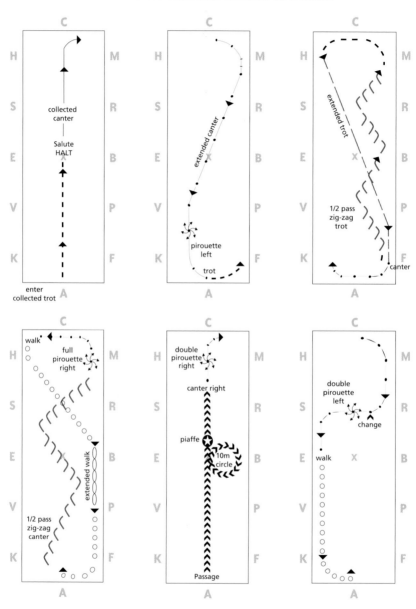

190

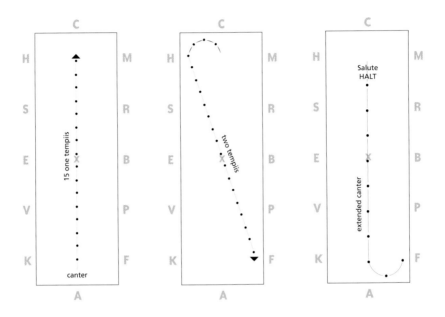

Grand Prix - 2000 Palm Beach Dressage Derby - Freestyle

Barbara Silverman and Chantor de Bounce

Music: Tarzan

Choreography: Tigger Montague/Spirit Horse Productions

1997 First Level Pas de Deux

Michael Matson and Delmaal
Theresa Cottle and Max

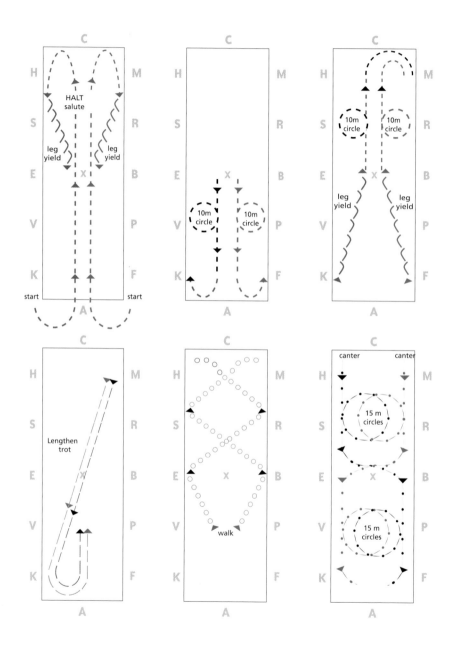

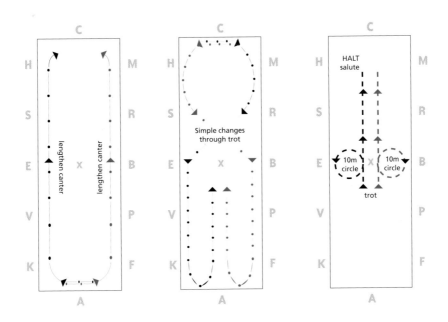

1997 First Level Pas de Deux

Michael Matson and Delmaal
Theresa Cottle and Max

Music: *New Jazz*
Choreography: *Leigh Ann Hazel-Groux*

1998 Prix St. George Pas de Deux

Ann DeMateo and Lotus
Kathy Kulick and Grandeur

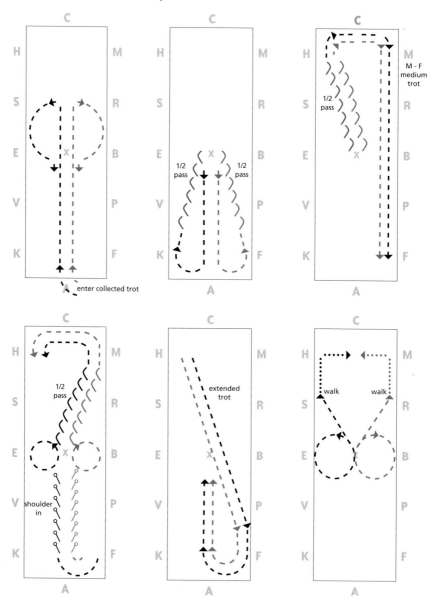

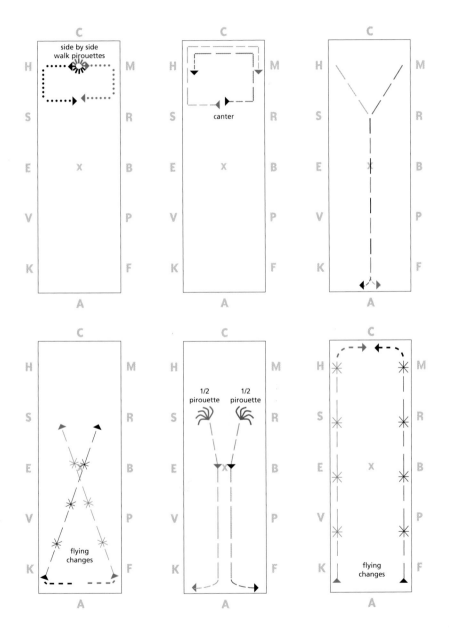

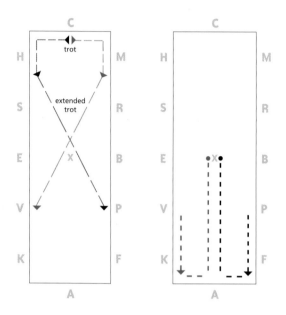

1998 Prix St. George Pas de Deux

Ann DeMateo and Lotus
Kathy Kulick and Grandeur

Music: *New Jazz*

   Arrangement by: Leigh Ann Hazel-Groux

Choreography: *Bent Jensen*